6.99

CU00764900

IMAGES
of Wales

THE SOUTH WALES BORDERERS
(24TH REGIMENT OF FOOT)
1881-1969

The Colour Party, 1st Battalion, 24th Regiment, after being presented to Queen Victoria at Osborne House on the Isle of Wight, 28 July 1880. Left to right: Col. J.M.G. Tongue (Commanding), Lt W. Weallens, Col.-Sgt Devery, Col.-Sgt Fallon, Col.-Sgt Wilson, Col.-Sgt Buttery, Lt A.B. Phipps, Cpl Roy DCM (Rorke's Drift). The Queen's colour (on the left) is the colour rescued from the Buffalo River after the disaster at Isandhlwana. The Queen attached to the colour a wreath of Immortelles – dried flowers – which was shortly afterwards replaced by a wreath made of silver.

IMAGES
of Wales

THE SOUTH WALES BORDERERS
(24TH REGIMENT OF FOOT)
1881-1969

Compiled by
Martin Everett
for the South Wales Borderers Museum

TEMPUS

First published 1999, reprinted 2002

Tempus Publishing Limited
The Mill, Brimscombe Port,
Stroud, Gloucestershire, GL5 2QG

The right of Martin Everett to be identified as the Author of this work has been
asserted by him in accordance with the Copyrights, Designs and Patents Act 1988.

British Library Cataloguing in Publication Data.
A catalogue record for this book is available from the British Library.

ISBN 0 7524 1846 7

Typesetting and origination by Tempus Publishing Limited
Printed in Great Britain by Midway Colour Print, Wiltshire

Contents

The Memorial to the 24th Regiment at Isandhlwana, Natal was unveiled by General Sir Reginald Hart VC KCB KCVO on 4 March 1914. The blessing was given by the Right Reverend W.L. Vyvyan, the Bishop of Zululand, who is standing on General Hart's right holding the white panama. The General, then commanding British troops in South Africa, was awarded the Victoria Cross while serving with the Royal Engineers in Afghanistan in 1879. Sadly, there were no members of the 24th Regiment present at the dedication ceremony.

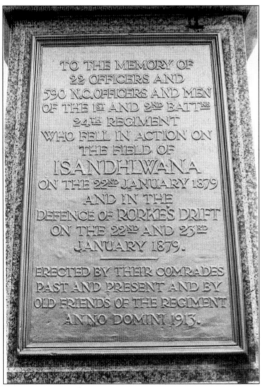

TO THE MEMORY OF
22 OFFICERS AND
590 N.C.OFFICERS AND MEN
OF THE 1ST AND 2ND BATTNS
24TH REGIMENT
WHO FELL IN ACTION ON
THE FIELD OF
ISANDHLWANA
ON THE 22ND JANUARY 1879
AND IN THE
DEFENCE OF RORKE'S DRIFT
ON THE 22ND AND 23RD
JANUARY 1879.

ERECTED BY THEIR COMRADES
PAST AND PRESENT AND BY
OLD FRIENDS OF THE REGIMENT
ANNO DOMINI 1913.

The plaque on the upper part of the memorial shows a date of 1913 not 1914.

Introduction

It is often said that if one gets off to a good start one never looks back. Dering's Regiment, later to become known as the 24th Regiment, is a good example of the truth in that saying. In March 1689, King William issued a commission to Sir Edward Dering to raise a Regiment of Foot, and in August that year the new regiment embarked for its first campaign in Ireland.

In February 1702, John Churchill, Duke of Marlborough – Commander-in-Chief of King William's forces on the Continent and one of England's greatest soldiers – took over as Colonel of the Regiment. The Regiment served throughout the War of the Spanish Succession and fought at the famous battles of Blenheim, Ramillies, Oudenarde and Malplaquet. Marlborough is said to be the first senior commander who really cared for the welfare of his troops. This Marlborough tradition, maintained over the years, has helped to foster the family spirit which has always been a marked feature of the Regiment and has led to many outstanding achievements and the award of twenty-three Victoria Crosses to its soldiers.

Following service in Canada and America, during the campaign for Independence, the 24th Regiment was instructed, in 1782, to style itself the 24th (2nd Warwickshire) Regiment of Foot, and it was under this title that the regiment was known for the next one hundred years. In June 1801 the 24th Regiment was sent to Egypt to reinforce the British force fighting the French. They arrived to take part in the capture of Alexandria which ended the campaign. The 24th, together with the other regiments involved, were awarded the Sphinx, superscribed 'Egypt' which was later an insignia on the Regimental Colour and the collar badge of the Regiment.

In September 1804, a 2nd Battalion was raised and took part in Wellington's great victories in Spain gaining nine Battle Honours for the Regiment. The most significant and hardest was Talavera in July 1809 when the 2nd/24th held their line, suffered many casualties but allowed the Foot Guards to reform in rear to secure victory for Wellington.

In 1849 the 1st Battalion of the 24th fought as part of General Sir Hugh Gough's Army of the Punjab at Chillianwallah in the Second Sikh War. Later in Queen Victoria's reign, both the 1st and 2nd Battalions of the 24th were engaged in the Zulu War of 1879. On 22 January five companies of the 1st Battalion and one company of the 2nd, in camp at Isandhlwana, were attacked by a great mass of Zulus. Surrounded and greatly outnumbered, they fought desperately but were finally overwhelmed when the supply of ammunition failed.

When it was evident that all was lost, Lts Melvill and Coghill were ordered to save the Queen's Colour of the 1st Battalion. They fought their way through to the Buffalo River, but it was there that both officers were killed. Fortunately, the Colour was later recovered from the muddy waters of the river and now hangs in the Regimental Chapel in Brecon Cathedral.

Meanwhile, 'B' Company 2/24th, under Lt Bromhead, was at Rorke's Drift, some 10 miles from the scene of the disaster. That same afternoon the victorious Zulus swept on and some 4,000 of them launched a series of fierce attacks on the tiny garrison at Rorke's Drift. The attacks continued until the early hours of the next morning but they were all beaten off. Eleven Victoria Crosses were awarded for this action: seven to members of the 24th Regiment – this is still the highest number of awards given for a single action. These events were so vividly brought to life again in Stanley Baker's 1964 film *Zulu*.

By 1873, the 24th Regiment was recruiting mainly from Welsh border counties and a Permanent Depot was established in Brecon. It was therefore logical that in 1881 when the infantry was given territorial titles, assuming the title of 'The South Wales Borderers'. Shortly after this the Volunteer Battalions of Monmouthshire, as well as those of Brecknock and Radnor, were affiliated to the Regiment.

After 'Black Week', in December 1899, the 2nd Battalion was sent to South Africa. The Anglo-Boer War also gave a first-ever chance for the Volunteer and Militia units of the South Wales Borderers of active overseas service. The success of the volunteers saw the creation of the Monmouthshire Regiment (TF), in 1908, from the 2nd, 3rd and 4th Volunteer Battalions.

In the First World War, the 24th raised eighteen Battalions, gained six Victoria Crosses and was awarded seventy-four Battle Honours. In 1914, on the other side of the world in China, the 2nd Battalion took part with the Japanese in the capture of the German Treaty Port of Tsingtao and thereby gained a Battle Honour unique in the British Army. In 1918, the 7th Battalion were awarded the French Croix de Guerre for their attack on the Grand Gouronné in Mesopotmia: only eleven units have been given this honour. The 2nd Monmouths had the distinction of being the first territorial unit to be allocated a battalion sector in the trenches in December 1914. At the end of the war they were the only territorial battalion to march into Germany.

The years between the wars were not particularly peaceful as both battalions were involved in the trouble spots of the Empire. During the Second World War the 2/24th had the distinction of being the only Welsh Battalion to land on the Normandy Beaches on D-Day. Together with the 2nd and 3rd Monmouths they fought throughout the North-West Europe Campaign until VE Day. The 6th Battalion was one of the outstanding battalions in Burma.

The post-war years saw the Regiment dealing with illegal Jewish immigrants in Palestine and Cyprus, curbing the Shifta's activities in Eritrea, fighting communist terrorists in Malaya and finally policing the Ma'alla district of Aden in 1967.

However, as a result of the 1967 Defence Review, drastic cuts in the armed forces were proposed and the Welsh Brigade was to be reduced by one battalion. Fortunately, an interchange of officers and senior ranks between regiments in the Brigade had occurred for many years. Therefore, the amalgamation of the South Wales Borderers with the Welch Regiment, although tinged with much sadness, enabled the newly formed Royal Regiment of Wales to capitalize immediately on the traditions and soldierly qualities of two fine Welsh Regiments.

The photographs, which form the contents of this book, are taken from the extensive regimental archives held at Brecon. The selection covers the period from 1881 to 1969 when this famous Regiment carried the name 'The South Wales Borderers'. I am very grateful that the Trustees have allowed many of them to be published for the first time. I sincerely hope that these images will be of interest to many people around the world who follow the fortunes of the 'Old 24th'.

Martin Everett
24th Regiment
South Wales Borderers Museum
Brecon 1999

One

Days of Empire
1881-1899

Battle Honour: BURMA 1885-87

1st Battalion

Colchester (1880-1882) – Manchester (1882-1883) – Kilkenny, Ireland (1883-1885) – Curragh, Ireland (1885-1886) – Birr, Ireland (1886-1887) – Dublin (1887-1889) – Aldershot (1889-1892) – Cairo, Egypt (1893-1895) – Gibraltar (1895-1897) – Meerut, India (1897-1898).

2nd Battalion

Secunderabad, India (1880-1883) – Bangalore, India (1884) – Madras, India (1884-1886) – Burma campaign (1886-1888) – Bureilly and Ranikhet, India (1888-1890) – Allahabad, India (1890-1892) – Aden (1892-1893) – Portsmouth & Gosport (1893-1895) – Aldershot, Hampshire (1895-1897) – Pembroke Dock (1897-1899).

Militia

The Royal South Wales Borderers Militia and the Royal Montgomery Militia became the 3rd and 4th (Militia) Battalions, South Wales Borderers.

Volunteers

The Rifle Volunteer units of Brecknockshire, Radnorshire and Monmouthshire became 1st (Brecknockshire), 2nd, 3rd and 4th Volunteer Battalion, South Wales Borderers. In 1897, the 5th Volunteer Battalion was raised in Montgomery and Cardiganshire.

The staff of 1st (Brecknockshire) Volunteer Battalion, South Wales Borderers, at Aldershot in 1885. Among those present are, left to right: QM A. Orlopp, Col. T. Conway Lloyd (Commanding), Capt. J.D.A.T. Lloyd SWB (Adjutant) and Sgt-Maj. D. Dickey (formerly of the Grenadier Guards).

The 2nd Battalion Instructors of Musketry, with Maj. Gonville Bromhead VC, in Burma in 1886. Maj. Bromhead died of euteric fever at Allahabad, India, on 9 February 1891. Col.-Sgt William Summers is sitting on the ground to the left of Maj. Bromhead.

Officers of the 3rd (Militia) Battalion at camp in Brecon in 1886. Left to right, back row: Capt. J.A. Norton (on tent), 2nd-Lt C.E.F. Walker, Mr C. de Winton, Lt F. Hyslop, Capt. H.A. Franklin, Capt. C. Healey, Lt W.W.G. Griffith, Lt R. Price, Lt T.C.B. Watkins. Front row: Capt. S.M. Thomas, Capt. T.W. Jones (lying), Lt H.V.S. Ormand, Maj. J.A.F. Snead, Lt Lea.

Colonel Glennie with the Non-Commissioned Officers then serving with the 1st Battalion in Dublin in 1888 who sailed with the SS *Clyde* arriving in South Africa on 3 April 1879 with a draft of 520 men to reinforce the 1st Battalion after the disaster at Isandhlwana. The draft included two guardsmen, one of whom is shown here on the right of the photograph.

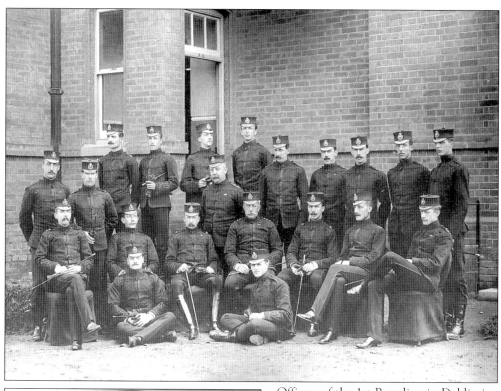

Officers of the 1st Battalion in Dublin in 1889. They are wearing undress flock jackets. Left to right, back row: Lt H.P. Pulliene, Lt C.E.F. Walker, 2nd-Lt Cleeve, Lt F.StJ. Hughes. Second row from the back: Lt A.C. Way, Lt C.A.R. Scott, QM & Capt. J.J. Tomkins, Capt. E.S. Gillman, Capt. J.D.A.T. Lloyd, Capt. B.W.S. Van Straubenzee, Lt S.F. Cooke, Lt J. Parker. Third row, seated: Capt. H.E. Every, Capt. G. Turner, Maj. H.G. Mainwaring, Col F. Glennie (Commanding), Lt H.G. Casson (Adjutant), Capt. F.C. King-Hunter, Capt Curll. Front row: Lt W.E.B. Smith, 2nd-Lt F.G.C.M. Morgan.

Col. Farquhar Glennie, one of the co-authors of the first regimental history, *Historical Records of the 24th Regiment*, which was published in 1892. This portrait was taken when he was commanding the 1st Battalion in 1892.

The bayonet fighting team of 'F' Company, 1st Battalion, who were overall winners of the Army Competition, Military Tournament at Aldershot in 1892. Capt. F.C. King Hunter is standing in the centre and Sgt James (team captain) is to the right of Capt. Hunter.

The 1st Battalion's return to the Sphinx, Egypt, in 1893. The 24th Regiment was awarded the Battle Honour of a Sphinx superscribed 'Egypt' on 6 July 1802, for helping to defeat Napoleon's Army in Egypt the previous year. The Sphinx is still one of the devices borne on the Regimental Colour of the Royal Regiment of Wales.

The 2nd Battalion marching past in line at Southsea Common, 1894. Lt-Col. E.S. Browne VC (mounted) is commanding.

Lt-Col. (later Brig.-Gen.) H.G. Mainwaring FRGS, in 1896. Born in India, Henry Mainwaring was commissioned to the 24th Foot in 1872, and saw service during the Zulu war. He was a noted big-game hunter which, in those days, was a pursuit that did not seem to interfere with a successful army career.

Lt W.L. Lawrence from Chepstow in 1896. Bill Lawrence was killed while leading 'C' Company, 1st Battalion, at Gheluvelt on 31 October 1914. His name is the first commemorated on the SWB panel on the Menin Gate, Ypres.

The Polo team of 1st Battalion, winners of the Gibraltar Cup, in 1896. The Battalion won the Infantry Polo Cup, Egypt, in 1894 and the Gibraltar Polo Cup in 1895, 1896 and 1897. It also won the Infantry Polo Cup, India, in 1898. Left to right: Capt. S.F. Cooke, Lt (later Maj-Gen.) W.E.B. Smith, Lt F.W. Gray, Capt. (later Brig.-Gen.) H.G. Casson.

The Band of the 1st Battalion in Gibraltar in 1896. Seated in the centre are: Sgt Blakeley, Lt C.E.F. Walker, Lt-Col. H.G. Mainwaring (Commanding), Lt B.W. Collier, Bandmaster J.O. Caborn.

1st Battalion tented camp at Ali Masgid. The battalion was marching all the way from Bombay to Meerut in India during 1897.

Cyclists of the 5th Volunteer Battalion at Towyn, Merioneth, with Lt C.E. Elwell (seated, centre) in 1897.

The 4th (Militia) Battalion on parade at Welshpool in 1897. The Regimental Colour has a white background reflecting the white facings of SWB uniforms introduced in 1881.

General Wodehouse and the Sergeants of the 2nd Battalion at Aldershot on 7 July 1897. Left to right, back row: L/Sgt Smith, Sgt Stevens, Sgt J. Evans, Sgt T. Evans, L/Sgt Charles, Sgt Laking. Second row from the back: Sgt Jones, Sgt Segers, Sgt Soper, Sgt Price, Sgt McLoughlin, Sgt Weaver. Third row: Sgt Stanborough, Sgt Connolly, Sgt Kavanagh, Sgt Shergold, Col.-Sgt Griffiths, L/Sgt Bowgett, L/Sgt Lloyd, Sgt Allcroft, Col.-Sgt Taylor. Fourth row: L/Sgt Overbuary, Sgt Morse, Sgt Wilson, Sgt Thomas, Pioneer Sgt Rayner, Col.-Sgt Holloway, Col.-Sgt Keppy, Sgt Lewis, L/Sgt Ruck, L/Sgt Erratt, Band Sgt Wright. Fifth row, sitting: Sgt Master Tailor Oliver, Ord.-Room Sgt Murphy, Sgt.-Instr of Musketry Powell, QMS Phelan, Sgt-Maj. Floyd, Col. R.A.P. Clements DSO ADC, General E. Wodehouse (Colonel of the Regiment), Major the Hon U. de R.B. Roche, Lt C.L. Taylor (Adjutant), Bandmaster O'Donnell, Sgt-Dmr Fry, Armr-Sgt Patrick, Sgt.-Master-Cook Fathers. Front row: Col.-Sgt Scott, Col.-Sgt Pryce, Col.-Sgt Morgan, Sgt Cobner, Col.-Sgt Parrington.

The seven VC holders from the 24th Regiment in Brecon for the unveiling the Zulu war memorial tablet in the Priory Church (later Brecon Cathedral) in January 1898. The group includes Pte Robert Jones who died in tragic circumstances eight months later. Left to right, back row: Ex-Pte R. Jones VC (Rorke's Drift), Sgt H. Hook VC (Rorke's Drift), Ex-Pte W. Jones VC (Rorke's Drift). Front row, sitting: Ex-Pte D Bell (Andaman Islands), Col. E.S. Browne VC (Khambula), Ex-Pte F. Hitch VC (Rorke's Drift), L/Cpl J Williams VC (Rorke's Drift).

Crickhowell Company, 1st (Brecknockshire) Volunteer Battalion, South Wales Borderers, at Glanusk Park with their Honorary Colonel, the Lord Glanusk VD, in 1898.

The display of Colours and Drums of the 2nd Battalion at the Regimental Ball, Pembroke Dock, on 13 October 1898. These Colours were presented to the 2nd Battalion by General the Lord Napier at Gibraltar in 1880. They replaced those lost at Isandhlwana and were carried by the 2nd Battalion until their disbandment in 1947 – for a total of sixty-seven years.

The 1st Battalion Subalterns (Riding) picnic party to Dosalli, India, on 31 December 1898. Left to right, back row: Lt R.P. Yates, Lt B.W. Collier, Miss Bancroft (sister of Mrs Cooke), Lt F.W. Gray, Miss Weston, 2nd-Lt D.G.B. Paton, Middle row: Mrs Collier, Mrs Cooke, Miss Turner, Miss Collier. Front row: 2nd Lt T.C. Greenway, Miss Cresswell (1), 2nd-Lt C.S. Stooks, Miss Cresswell (2), Lt T.P. Melville, Lt H.W. Stevens (and dog).

Sergeants of the 5th Volunteer Battalion at Porthcawl Camp, 1899. Only some of the names are known. Left to right, second row: Col.-Sgt Inst. Lichfield, QM & Hon.-Lt W.F. Richards, Col.-Sgt Edwards, Col.-Sgt Astley, Col.-Sgt O'Malley, Capt & Adjt C.E.F. Walker, Col.-Sgt Jones. Front row: Col.-Sgt Inst. Hodge, ORS Jones, Sgt-Maj. L. Gibson, Sgt Bugler Pritchard, Col.-Sgt Inst. Hemmings.

A tea party for the 5th Volunteer Battalion outside the Adjutant's tent, Porthcawl Camp, in 1899. Left to right: Capt. C. Wadsworth, Lt C.E. Elwell, Capt. E.W. Kirkby, -?-, Miss Fichener, Capt. C.E.F. Walker, 2nd-Lt G.W.H. Wakefield, Capt. Sir William Lennox Napier Bt., Lt H.A. Kirkby.

Officers and NCOs of 'C' Company, 1st Battalion, Chakrata, India, in 1899. Left to right, back row: Cpl Day, L/Sgt Davies, Sgt Case, Front row, sitting: Sgt Halford, Col.-Sgt Instr Musketry Erskine, Lt T.C. Greenway, Capt. C.A.R. Scott, 2nd-Lt D.G. Johnson, Col.-Sgt Berryman, Sgt Morse. Lying at the front: Cpl Basp, Cpl Jolnson.

The dogs of the 1st Battalion outside Colonel Henry Mainwaring's bungalow, Chakrata, India, in 1899. Left to right: Mrs Mainwaring (with Binks), Maj. C.E. Curll, Lt C.E. Kitchen (with Batcha), Lt T.C. Greenway (with Satan), Capt. W.E.B. Smith (with Piper, father of the other three dogs).

Officers from the 2nd Battalion, Richmond Barracks, Dublin, in November 1899. Left to right: Maj. the Hon U. de R.B. Roche (Second in Command), Col. R.A.P. Clements DSO ADC (Commanding), Lt C.L. Taylor (Adjutant), Sgt-Maj. H. Floyd.

Two
Prelude to War
1900-1914

Battle Honour: SOUTH AFRICA 1900-1902

1st Battalion

Chakrata, India (1898-1899) – Dehra Dun and Pur, India (1899-1900) – Meerut, India (1900) – Peshawar, India (1900-1902) – Mian Mir and Umballa, India (1902) – Delhi, India (1902-1903) – Mian Mir and Dalhousie, India (1903-1905) – Karachi and Hyderabad, India (1905-1909) – Quetta, India (1909-1910) – Chatham, Kent (1910-1913) – Bordon, Hampshire (1913-1914).

2nd Battalion

Dublin (1899-1900) – Anglo-Boer War and South Africa (1900-1904) – Bulford, Wiltshire (1904) – Tidworth, Wiltshire (1904-1906) – Aldershot, Hampshire (1906-1909) – Chatham, Kent (1909-1910) – Pretoria, South Africa (1911-1912) – Tientsin, China (1912-1914).

Militia Battalions

The 3rd (Militia) Battalion volunteered to serve overseas during the Anglo-Boer war. In April 1908, the 3rd (Militia) Battalion became the 3rd (Special Reserve) Battalion and 4th (Militia) Battalion was disbanded.

Volunteer Battalions

All five battalions provided volunteers to serve with 2nd Battalion, South Wales Borderers, during the Anlgo-Boer war and gained the Battle Honour, SOUTH AFRICA 1900-02, for the Volunteers. In the Haldane reforms of April 1908, the 1st Volunteer Battalion became The Brecknockshire Battalion, South Wales Borderers TF. The 2nd, 3rd, and 4th Volunteer Battalions were renamed to become the 1st, 2nd, and 3rd Battalions, The Monmouthshire Regiment TF. The 5th Volunteer Battalion was also renamed to become the 7th Battalion, Royal Welch Fusiliers TF. Colours were presented the Brecknocks, 2nd and 3rd Battalions, The Monmouthshire Regiment, in Windsor Great Park in 1909. The 1st Monmouths following the Rifle Regiment's tradition carried no Colours.

The 1st Battalion Active Service Volunteer Company at Brecon Barracks prior to sailing to South Africa in January 1900. The selected volunteers from all five Volunteer Battalions served with the 2nd Battalion until October 1900. The building shown is now the South Wales Borderers Museum.

The Volunteers who were to serve overseas in South Africa with the 2nd Battalion came from the 5th Volunteer Battalion at Brecon Barracks in January 1900. They included Lt H.A. Kirkby, Sgt J.T. Astley and Col E.L. Jones sitting in the centre.

Staff of 'E' Company, 5th Volunteer Battalion, at Aberystwyth in 1900. In 1908 this company became part of the 7th Battalion, the Royal Welch Fusiliers, and subsequently Aberystwyth University Officers' Training Corps. Left to right, back row: Sgt F.R. Parkes, L/Sgt H.J. Edwards, Sgt D.S. Jennings, Front row: Col.-Sgt F. Betts (Permanent Staff), Capt. J.R. Ainsworth Davis, 2nd-Lt J.W. Marshall, Col.-Sgt J.P. Millington.

The Colour Sergeants of the 1st Battalion at Meerut, India, in 1901. Left to right, back row: Col.-Sgt Murphy ('C' Coy), Col.-Sgt Morgan ('B' Coy), Col.-Sgt Price ('A' Coy), Col.-Sgt Berryman ('G' Coy), Front row: Col.-Sgt Fryers ('H' Coy), Sgt-Maj. J. Wilson, Col.-Sgt O'Leary ('E' Coy), Col. C.V. Trower (Commanding), Lt T.P. Melvill (Assistant Adjutant), Col.-Sgt Holley ('F' Coy), Col.-Sgt Lott ('D' Coy). The Colours are those carried by the Battalion during the 1879 Zulu campaign. Lt Mevill is the son of Lt Teignmouth Melvill VC who saved the Queen's Colour after Isandhlwana.

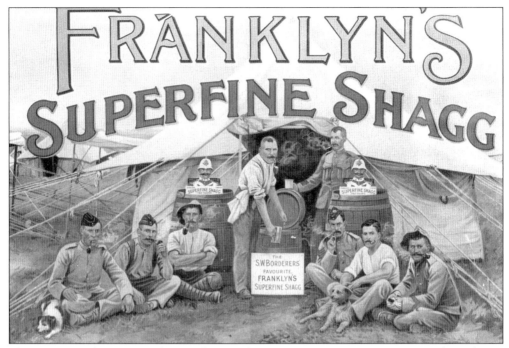

The Regimental Canteen during the Anglo-Boer war 1900-1902. Interestingly, tobacco advertising was not subject to a health warning in those days.

Officers of 5th Volunteer Battalion at Porthcawl Camp in 1902. The non-regulation cockades in their slouch hats are probably influenced by some officers who had previously served with Montgomeryshire Yeomanry. Left to right, back row: A/Chaplain W.M. Roberts, Lt J.W. Marshall, Lt J.M. Howell, Capt. A.W. Pryce-Jones, Capt. C. Wadsworth, 2nd-Lt J.J. Sudborough, Capt. G.W.H. Wakefield, QM & Hon.-Lt W.F. Richards. Front row: Capt. W.H. Pitten (Bde Staff), Bde.-Surg. P.E. Hill VD, Lt-Col. G.A. Hutchings VD, Col. Sir A.P. Vivian KCB VD (Comd South Wales Border Bde), Lt-Col. E. Pryce-Jones MP (Comd 5VB SWB), Col. C.G.C. Money CB (Comd 24th Regt Dist), Capt. & Adjt. C.E.F. Walker, Lt-Col. R.D. Garnons-Williams (Bde Major), Capt. Sir William Napier Bt. Lt C.E. Elwell is lying on ground.

Sergeants of the 1st Battalion South Wales Borderers and 2nd Battalion Welch Regiment enjoy each other's company at the Delhi Durbar in January 1903.

Col. C.V. Trower, a legendary figure in the 24th Regiment. He served in the Zulu and Anglo-Boer wars and commanded the 1st Battalion in India, 1901-1905. At the age of fifty-nine, he rejoined to serve in the trenches commanding the 5th (Pioneer) Battalion from 1914-18. This portrait photograph was taken in 1904.

Lt (later Air Commodore) A.G. Board, in 1904, soon after he joined the Regiment. In November 1910, against Army orders, he took fifteen days' leave to learn to fly with Louis Bleriot's flying school at Hendon. He was rewarded with Pilot's Certificate No. 36 and a rocket from his Commanding Officer! He retired from the RAF as Chief of the Air Staff, Middle East in 1931.

Dalhousie Theatricals with the 1st Battalion in India in 1904.

A wedding party of a Lance Corporal of the 1st Battalion in Dalhousie, 1904. Sadly, no names are recorded. The soldiers are wearing the serge flock jackets with white facings issued in India at the time. The Regiment would return to their traditional 24th green facings in the following year.

Sgt-Maj. C. Hawkshaw and his Colour Sergeants, 1st Battalion, in Dalhousie, 1904. A Colour Sergeant was the senior NCO in each company at this time; the appointment of Company Sergeant Major was not introduced until the First World War. The Colours shown are those from the Zulu war. Sgt-Maj. Hawkshaw rejoined in 1914 to become Regimental Sergeant Major of the 5th (Service) Battalion.

Drummers of the 2nd Battalion wearing Brodrick caps in 1905. They are, left to right: L/Cpl Leeke, Dmrs Marsh, Tricker and Bruce.

Capt. WL Lawrence (Adjutant) from the 'B' Coy, 1st Battalion, hockey team in Karachi, India, in 1905. Note the Welsh Dragon and Sphinx Badge on hockey shirts.

The 1st Battalion silver in 1905. The collection includes the magnificent Duke of Marlborough centrepiece commissioned for the Regiment's bicentenary in 1889.

The 1866 Colours of 1st Battalion – Zulu war Colours with the Fleming Drum Major's Silver Staff – in 1905. The drum shells have a painted white background to reflect the uniform facing colours worn at that time.

The 1st Battalion on parade at Karachi, 1906.

Motor cars belonging to the 2nd Battalion at Tidworth in July 1905. Two very early Rolls-Royce cars were sold to South Wales Borderers Officers. This one, registered A-8528, belonged to Lt H.C.H.W. Moffat. Left to right are: Capt. F.W. Gray, Lt H.C.H.W. Moffat, 2nd-Lt D.G. Johnson, 2nd-Lt J. Bradstock, Capt. C.E. Morgan (with Tattie, the regimental dog), Lt W.C. Curgenven, Lt G.H. Birkett (with the regimental motor), Lt E.H.A. Hodgson.

The 1st Battalion Regimental 'Potted' sports, 1906. A 'Potted' sports day gave soldiers an opportunity to dress up or to dress down. Winners of the various competitions were usually rewarded with bottles of beer.

A triumphal arch erected by the 1st Battalion at Karachi, India for the visit of TRH The Prince and Princess of Wales (later HM King George V and HM Queen Mary) in October 1906. The words were in English on the other side of the arch!

Lt B.W. Collier was born in Broughty Ferry, Scotland and was commissioned in the South Wales Borderers in 1895. He served in the 2nd Battalion and with the Mounted Infantry in the Anglo-Boer war. In the First World War he served with the 1st Battalion and later commanded the 14th Battalion Royal Welch Fusiliers with whom he won a DSO. At the end of the war, he commanded the 51st Battalion South Wales Borderers as part of the army of occupation in Germany.

The 1st Battalion, Aldershot Review, on Laffan's Plain in 1907. Maj. C.E.F. Walker is seen in front of the No. 1 Guard.

Pte Driscoll, 2nd Battalion, wearing the unpopular Brodrick cap with two regimental wildebeest at Aldershot in 1907. The wildebeest were brought back from South Africa in 1903. One survived and was returned to South Africa in 1910.

Officers of the 2nd Battalion at Aldershot in 1907. Left to right, back row: QM & Hon.-Lt H. Floyd, Sgt.-Maj. G. Rayner. Front row: Maj. H.M. Graham (Second-in Command), Lt-Col. C.E. Curll (Commanding), Capt. W.C. Curgenven (Adjutant), Lt D.G. Johnson (Assistant Adjutant).

Colours of the 2nd Battalion, Officers' Mess, Oudenarde Barracks, at Aldershot in 1907. Draped over the drums is the Colour purchased from the Marquis de St George in Paris in 1894. It was claimed to be the 2nd Battalion's Regimental Colour lost at Isandhlwana. However, after careful investigation and thorough examination, it was decided that the Colour was not genuine.

A wedding reception party of 6315 Sgt Hughie Marr, an instructor on the staff of the SWB Depot, to Miss Emily Rothero at the Market Tavern, Brecon, on 11 September 1907. At the outbreak of war, in August 1914, Hughie Marr was Sergeant-Major of the 3rd (Special Reserve) Battalion. He was immediately commissioned and went on to command a service battalion of the Cheshire Regiment. For his war services he was awarded the OBE and MC and retired as a Lieutenant-Colonel.

The Band of 2nd Battalion, Aliwal Barracks, Tidworth, 1906. The band are just reverting to the traditional 24th green facings on their uniforms, but are still wearing the Brodrick caps which were phased out at about this time. The band numbers are 49! In the centre seated left to right: Sgt Cairnes, Bandmaster P. O'Donnell, Captain A.J. Reddie (Adjutant), Lt-Col C.E. Curll (Commanding), 2Lt J. Bradstock (Assistant Adjutant), Band Sgt O'Donnell, Sgt James.

'H' Coy team, 2nd Battalion, under the command of Lt R.S. Gwynn, taking part in the Evelyn Wood March and Shoot Competition at Aldershot in 1908. Lt Gwynn served with the 1st Battalion during the First World War commanding the Battalion for a short period in 1915. He was awarded the DSO in 1916.

The 2nd Battalion marching past Field Marshal Sir George White VC, at the King's birthday parade, Laffan's Plain, Aldershot in 1908.

The Sergeants of the 2nd Battalion at Aldershot, 1909. Left to right, back row: Sgt Pearson, L/Sgt Edwards, Sgt Cresswell, L/Sgt James, L/Sgt Johnson, Sgt Clifford, L/Sgt Letton, L/Sgt Rees, Sgt Enright, Sgt Tring. Second row from the back: Sgt Cooling, Sgt Shergold, L/Sgt Leach, L/Sgt Hitch, L/Sgt Gould, Sgt Perkins, Sgt Brown, Sgt Herbert, Sgt Gillett, Sgt Moses. Third row: Sgt Allcroft, Sgt Millichamp, Sgt Humphries, Sgt Biddiss, Sgt Casey, Armr-Sgt Whitehouse, Sgt Press, Sgt Woods, L/Sgt Bean, Sgt Alabaster, Sgt Bryan, Sgt Higgins. Fourth row: Col.-Sgt Longstaffe, Col.-Sgt Davies, Sgt Wilson, Sgt Ellis, Sgt Randall, Sgt Britten, QMS (ORS) Albutt, Sgt Heal, Col.-Sgt Vaughan, Col.-Sgt Shirley, Sgt Dmr Matthews. Front row: Col.-Sgt Ross, Col.-Sgt Westlake, Sgt-Maj. Rayner, Maj. G. Going, Col. J.H. du B. Travers (Commanding), Lt & Adjt D.G. Johnson, QMS Stanborough, Col.-Sgt Spooner, Col.-Sgt Hulbert. Many of these sergeants later saw service in China, Gallipoli and on the Western Front during the First World War.

One of the most spectacular sets of drums ever manufactured, produced for 1st Battalion. Made in Sterling Silver by Messrs Potter & Co., of Aldershot, seen in 1908. The set consists of one bass, two tenor and twelve side drums. The heraldry, consisting of the Royal Arms, title, three badges, and nineteen honours are raised from the Sterling silver shell in repousse work. The cost was said to be in four figures and caused questions to be asked in Parliament – however, the set was a private purchase by the officers of the 24th Regiment. The green/white hatching on the drum hoops was exclusive to the 1st Battalion.

'F' Company, 2nd Battalion, winners of the Evelyn Wood March and Shoot Competition, at Aldershot in 1909. Field Marshal Sir Evelyn Wood VC introduced this competition when he commanded troops in Aldershot in the period, 1889-93. Left to right, back row: Pte Walters, Pte Mullins, L/Cpl Hurst, Pte Turner, Pte Haddon, Pte Loveridge. Second row from the back: Pte Woodham, Pte Crompton, Pte Ewens, Pte Evans, Pte Williams, Pte Freeman, L/Cpl Loveridge, L/Cpl Goldberg, Pte Fitzjohn. Third row: L/Cpl Warchus, Pte Cornick, Col.-Sgt Shirley, Maj. M.J.B.P. Beresford (Commanding), Lt E.H.A. Hodgson, Lt G.T.J. Barry (Captain of team), Cpl Mackay, Pte Groves. Front row, sitting: Pte Lambie, Pte Bissenden.

Officers and ladies of the 2nd Battalion, The Monmouthshire Regiment TF, at camp in Ammanford on August 1909. Left to right, back row: Capt. G.B.C. Ward (Adjutant), Col. Herbert MVO, Capt. J. Williams, Capt. J.G. Broackes, -?-, Capt. I. Evans, -?-. Second row from the back: -?-, Mr Courtis, Maj. (QM) A. Sale, Surg. E.M. Griffiths, Lt-Col. H.D. Griffiths, Maj. C.D. Lewis, Col. Rees (6th Welch), -?-, Maj. Sillery, Maj. P.G. Pennymore, Maj. E.J. Morris, Mr J. Cory. Third row, seated: Mr L. Forestier-Walker, Mr W.H. Jones, Mr L. Morgan (Lord Mayor of Cardiff), Mrs Jones, Col. J.A. Bradney, Col. Banfield (Bde Commander), -?-, Lt E. Jenkins, Miss Jones, Mr Menton. Front row, on the ground: Capt. J.C. Jenkins, -?-, Lt H.W.E. Bailey, Lt R.A. Hobbs, Lt M. Watkins, Mr Jones, Lt H.T. Edwards.

The 1st Battalion bivouacking during Brigade training at Longmoor Camp, Hampshire, 1909.

The first gathering of the Old Comrades Club, Oudenarde Barracks, Aldershot, on 23 January 1909 on the 30th anniversary of Rorke's Drift. In the front are three veterans of Rorke's Drift, left to right: Major Frank Bourne DCM, Pte Frederick Hitch VC and Pte John Williams VC.

'To your Colour, Present Arms!' The 2nd Battalion mounting King's Guard at Wellington Barracks, London, under command of Maj. J. Going on 23 August 1910.

The proclamation of the accession of King George V at the Shirehall, Brecon, on 7 May 1910. The event was attended by staff and recruits from the Depot, South Wales Borderers.

Officers and Senior NCOs, 1st Battalion, The Monmouthshire Regiment TF, wearing their dark green rifle brigade uniforms, c. 1910.

5441 Sgt-Maj. George Rayner, 2nd
Battalion (1906-1911), wearing two
medals: the Queen's South Africa Medal
(clasps: Johannesburg, Cape Colony,
Orange Free State, South Africa 1901)
and the Long Service & Good Conduct
Medal in 1910.

The Brecon Hunt 'Meet' in the Barracks
in February 1921. The view of the
Officers' Mess remains largely unchanged
today. The Regimental Sergeant Major
on the left is William Bruntnell.

The 2nd Battalion on Guard Duty in Teintsin, China, in the winter of 1913.

The 2nd Battalion Regimental boxing competition, Tientsin, China, in 1913.

Three

The Great War
1914-1918

South Wales Borderers

Seventy-four Battle Honours, of which ten are worn on the Queen's Colour: MONS, MARNE 1914, YPRES 1914-17-18, GHELUVELT, SOMME 1916-18, CAMBRAI 1917-18, DOIRAN 1917-18, LANDING AT HELLES, BAGHDAD, TSINGTAO.

1st Battalion

Proceeded with 1st Division, Expeditionary Force, overseas on 12 August 1914, and served in France throughout the war.

2nd Battalion

Present at the siege of Tsingtao, China, in 1914, then joined the 29th Division and went the Dardanelles where it took part in the original landing. Served throughout the Gallipoli campaign and then went with the 29th Division to France until the end of the war.

3rd Battalion (Reserve)

Provided drafts for Battalions on active service and were based near Liverpool throughout the war.

4th (Service) Battalion

Proceeded to Gallipoli with 13th Division in July 1915. In January 1916, returned to Egypt, and in March 1916 went to Mesopotamia, took part in the attempt to relieve Kut, and remained in Mesopotamia till the end of the war.

5th (Pioneer) Battalion

Divisional Pioneers of 19th Division. Went to France in July 1915 and served there until the end of the war.

6th (Pioneer) Battalion

Divisional Pioneers of 25th Division. Went to France in September 1915 and served there until the end of the war. In 1918, transferred to 30th Division.

7th (Service) Battalion

Went to France with 22nd Division in September 1915, latter transferred with this Division to Macedonia, where it served till the end of the war. In September 1918, the Battalion was awarded the Croix de Guerre by the French Government for conspicuous service in the attack on the Grand Couronné.

8th (Service) Battalion
Went to France with 22nd Division in September 1915 and was later transferred with this Division to Macedonia where it served till the end of the war.

9th (Service) Battalion
A Reserve Battalion which found drafts for Active Service Battalions.

10th (Service) Battalion
Known as 1st Gwent. Went to France with 38th (Welsh) Division and served there till the end of the war.

11th (Service) Battalion
Known as 2nd Gwent. Went to France with 38th (Welsh) Division and served there till the end of the war.

12th (Service) Battalion
Known as 3rd Gwent. A bantam battalion which went to France in June 1916 with the 40th Division and was disbanded in February 1918.

13th Battalion
Formed in July 1915 to find drafts for the 10th and 11th Battalions. Saw no active service.

14th Battalion
Formed in September 1915 to find drafts for Active Service Battalions. Never saw active service.

51st, 52nd and 53rd ('Young Soldiers') Battalions
Formed in 1918 and proceeded to the Rhine as part of the Army of Occupation.

1st Brecknockshire Battalion TF
Proceeded to Aden in 1915, where they earned the Battle Honour ADEN, and later went on to Mhow, India, where they remained till the end of the war. The 2nd and 3rd Line Battalions of Brecknocks were formed during the war for draft finding. Never saw active service.

The Monmouthshire Regiment
Twenty-two Battle Honours, of which ten are worn on the Queen's Colour: YPRES 1915-17-18, ST. JULIEN, SOMME 1916, ARRAS 1917, SCAPE 1917, LLANGEMARCK 1917, CAMBRAI 1917-18, HINDENBURG LINE, FRANCE AND FLANDERS 1914-18, ADEN.

1st Battalion TF
Joined 28th Division in France in February 1915. Became Divisional Pioneers for 46th Division in August 1915. Formed 2nd and 3rd line battalions during the War for training and for draft finding purposes. Never saw active service.

2nd Battalion TF
Joined 4th Division in France in November 1914. Became Divisional Pioneers for 29th Division in April 1916. Formed 2nd and 3rd line battalions during the War for training and for draft finding purposes. Never saw active service.

3rd Battalion TF
Joined 28th Division in France in February 1915. Became Divisional Pioneers of 49th Division in August 1915. Formed 2nd and 3rd line battalions during the War for training and for draft finding purposes. Never saw active service.

4th Battalion TF
Formed in June 1915 as 48th Provisional Battalion from home service personnel of Monmouthshire and Herefordshire. On 1 January 1917 it was redesigned 4th Battalion, The Monmouthshire Regiment. Spent most of the time in East Anglia. Never saw active service.

The boys of the Old Brigade at the SWB Depot, Brecon, in 1914. Standing, left to right: Sgt Honan (40½yrs) CQMS J Harris (40½yrs), Col.-Sgt Lambert (46 yrs), Col.-Sgt Rallison (41½years). Sitting: Capt. (QM) T. Murray (38 yrs), Col. F.C. King Hunter (38½yrs), Sgt-Maj. H. Andrews (39½yrs).

Officers of the 2nd Battalion in Hong Kong, after the successful action against the German held port of Tsingtao in November 1914. Left to right, back row: Lt C.M. Tippetts, Lt E.K. Laman (Quartermaster), Lt W. Rawle, Lt M.C. Morgan, Lt A.N. Cahusac, Lt R.L. Petre, Lt A.E. Williams, Lt C.B. Habershon, 2nd-Lt R.P. Behrens, Capt. D.H.S. Somerville, 2nd-Lt C.R. MacGregor. Front row: Capt. A.H.J. Ellis, Capt. J. Bradstock, Capt. T.C. Greenway, Maj. E.C. Margesson, Maj. J. Going, Lt-Col. H.G. Casson (Commanding), Maj. E.W. Jones, Capt. R.G. Palmer, Capt. G.H. Birkett (Adjutant), Capt. D.G. Johnson.

Officers of the 1st Battalion at Bordon, prior to their departure with the British Expeditionary Force to France at part of the 1st Division in 1914. Left to right. back row: Lt H.D. Dawes, Lt M.G. Richards, Lt A.E.L. James, 2nd-Lt J.R. Homfray (killed on 11 November 1914), Lt R.B. Hadley (killed on 31 October 1914), Lt C.W. Anstey, Lt J.M.L. Vernon. Middle row: Lt J.C. Coker (killed on 26 September 1914), Lt M.T. Johnson (died of wounds on 17 September 1914), Lt C.K. Steward, Lt H.H. Travers (died of wounds on 28 March 1915), Lt V.B. Ramsden, Lt C.J. Paterson (Adjutant) (died of wounds on 1 November 1914), Lt W.R. Wilson (Quartermaster), 2nd-Lt C.A. Baker, 2nd-Lt N.G. Silk (killed Gallipoli on 9 June 1915), 2nd-Lt C.C. Sills (killed on 25 September 1914). Front row: Capt. W.C. Curgenven (killed on 21 October 1914), Capt. G.B.C. Ward, Capt. F.G. Lawrence DSO, Capt. Elliott (Medical Officer), Major A.J. Reddie, Lt-Col. H.E.B. Leach (Commanding), Maj. W.L. Lawrence (killed on 31 October 1914), Maj. G.E.E. Welby (killed on 29 September 1914), Capt. W.O. Prichard (wounded on 26 September 1914, lost a leg), Capt. R.S. Gwynn, Capt. M.E. Yeatman (killed on 19 September 1914).

Officers of the 2nd Battalion relaxing after the successful operation at Tsingtao, China, in November 1914. Left to right: Maj. E.W. Jones, Capt. J. Bradstock, Lt C.B. Habersham, Capt. T.C. Greenway, Capt. G.H. Dive (doctor), Capt. D.G. Johnson.

The SWB Depot Band and Staff passing the
Shire Hall on their return from Church Parade
in Brecon, c. 1914. The officer marching behind
the Band is Captain (QM) Thomas Murray.

The 2nd Monmouths in the trenches at Le
Bizet, April 1915. Lt T.E.R. Williams is in the
foreground. The cut-out head of German Kaiser
was used to promote German sniper practice.

The 2nd Monmouths in the trenches at Le Bizet enjoying a food parcel from home, April 1915.

A view over the top for the 2nd Monmouths in the trenches at Le Bizet, April 1915.

The 2nd Monmouths in the trenches at Le Bizet, April 1915.

'B' Company, 2nd Monmouths, in the trenches at Le Bizet, April 1915. The 'SB' arm badge indicates a stretcher-bearer.

No. 14 Platoon, 8th (Service) Battalion, after a Church Parade at Hastings in January 1915. The Battalion sailed to France in September 1915 and later saw service in Macedonia. Front row, left to right: L/Cpl ?, Sgt J. Cuffe, Lt C.C. Woolley (Platoon Commander), Sgt Cox (Platoon Sergeant), L/Cpl ?. Lt Wooley later became Sir Charles Wooley and was Governor and Commander-in-Chief, Cyprus, when the 1st Battalion was stationed on the island, 1946-49. Sgts Cox and Cuffe had both seen previous service in the Anglo-Boer war.

Capt. 'Charlie' Pritchard, who was killed in action following a successful patrol into No Man's Land while serving with 12th Battalion on the Somme on 14 August 1916. Charlie Pritchard played club rugby for Newport and was capped fourteen times for Wales. He played in the famous 1905 match at Cardiff when Wales beat the New Zealand All Blacks, 3-0.

Maj. H.C. Rees from Ashford in Kent who was killed in action while serving with 12th Battalion (3rd Gwent) on 5 August 1916. Harry Rees worked for a firm of stockbrokers in Cardiff before taking a post in Alexandria in Egypt. He was a notable tennis player and was one of the men's doubles lawn tennis champions of Egypt.

'B' Company, 2nd Monmouths, Hampton Camp Bivouacs, Bleuet Farm, Belgium, 23 September 1917. Left to right, back row: Sgt A.J. Phelps, Sgt C. Hayes MSM, Sgt Dowle, Sgt J. Counsell, Middle row: Sgt J. Skinner, CSM C.H. Lock MM. Front row: CQMS S. Glover, CSM W.J. Bowen DCM, Sgt D.J. O'Leary, Sgt A.E. Turner MM.

Officers from the 2nd Monmouths on the Western Front, 28 May 1917. Left to right, back row: -?-, Major C. Comley. Middle row: Lt-Col. J. Evans (Commanding). Front row, sitting: Capt. ?, Capt. Leighton RAMC.

Maj. Christopher Comley MC, 2nd Monmouths, on the Western Front, 28 May 1917.

1st Brecknocks, winners of the All India (Calcutta) Rugby Challenge Cup, in 1917. Left to right, back row: QMS D. Williams (trainer), Pte A. Adams, L/Cpl D. Davies, Pte W.J. Harper, Pte J.W. Waite, Pte P. Williams, Cpl T. Jenkins, Sgt D. Martin, Sgt T.H. Davies. Middle row: Pte J.R. Thomas, L/Cpl E. Powell, L/Cpl S.C. Williams (captain of the team), Maj. A.L. Careless (Commanding), Capt. W.R. Lewis, L/Cpl W. Taylor (vice captain), Sgt J. Powell, Pte W.H. Williams. Front row: Pte A. Williams, Pte W.M. Watkins.

Officers of the 5th (Pioneer) Battalion at Bourecq in March 1917. They are wearing pioneer collar badges in addition to the SWB sphinx. Included are: 2nd-Lt R.T. Price, 2nd-Lt A.H. Moore (killed in action on 26 March 1918), 2nd-Lt W.K. Runham, 2nd-Lt L.V. Kent (died of wounds on 31 July 1917).

Representatives from the Depot, 24th Regiment, who attended the celebrations at Coleford, Forest of Dean, to mark the award of the Victoria Cross to Captain Angus Buchanan MC 4/SWB on 9 November 1917. Left to right, back row: L/Cpl M. Stevens MM, Sgt T. Press, CSM F. Kennington MM, Sgt G.S. Duffy DCM, Cpl J. Hatherton MM. Front row: CSM S.D. Bean DCM, CSM G. West DCM, RSM H.B. Andrews, Pte J. Williams VC, CSM F. Habberfield MC.

Sgt Ivor Rees VC of Llanelli. Ivor Rees won the Victoria Cross at Pilckem Ridge in July 1917 by personally charging a machine gun position and then a nearby enemy pill-box capturing two German officers and thirty men.

The 1st Battalion at Florin, Belgium, under the command of Lt-Col. C.L. Taylor DSO while on the march to Germany on 28 November 1918.

Survivors who went to France in 1914, still serving in the 1st Battalion in 1918. Left to right, back row: CSM G. Saunders MM, Pte C. Bartlett MM, Sgt A.E. Ravenhill MM, -?-, CSM H.G. House DCM. Front row: RSM J. Shirley MC, Sgt G. Gibbs MM.

Headquarter Company, 1st Battalion, Germany, November 1918. Front row, left to right (wearing Sam Browne belts): RSM J. Shirley MC, Capt. O.M. Wales MC, Lt-Col. C.L. Taylor DSO, Lt-Col. (QM) G.C. Thomas DSO. The others are not known.

CSM J.H. Williams VC DCM MM of Ebbw Vale. Jack Williams of 'B' Company was awarded the Victoria Cross for conspicuous bravery on 7/8 October 1918 during the 10th Battalion's attack on Villers Outreaux. On 22 February 1919 at Buckingham Palace he was decorated with four gallantry awards at the same investiture – VC, DCM, MM and bar.

Four
Between the Wars
1918-1939

South Wales Borderers

1st Battalion
Canterbury (1919) – Brecon (1919) – Chatham, Kent (1919) – Blackdown, Hampshire (1919-1920) – Dublin, Ireland (1920) – Dunhaughlin, Co. Meath (1920-1922) – Blackdown, Hampshire (1922-1923) – Devonport (1923-1927) – Lichfield (1927-1928) – Cairo (1928-1930) – Hong Kong (1930-1934) – (New Colours 28 March 1933) – Rawalpindi, India (1934-1938) – Waziristan Emergency (1937) – Landi Kotal, North West Frontier (1938-1939).

2nd Battalion
Brecon (1919) – Barrackpore and Dum-Dum, India (1919-1927) – Aden (1927-1929) – Portsmouth (1929-1932) – Catterick, Yorkshire (1932-1935) – Malta (1935-1936) – Palestine emergency (1936) – Londonderry, Northern Ireland (1936-1939).

The Monmouthshire Regiment TA

In 1922 the pre-war Territorial Force was re-constituted as the Territorial Army. The three battalions of the Monmouthshire Regiment returned, but the Brecknockshire Battalion was absorbed into the 3rd Battalion, The Monmouthshire Regiment TA. In 1938, the 1st (Rifle) Battalion, The Monmouthshire Regiment, became a Royal Artillery Searchlight Regiment and ceased to belong to the Corps of the South Wales Borderers.

The 2nd Battalion Colour Party at Burscheid, Germany, on 30 January 1919. The Colours were brought from Brecon especially for the occasion. Front row, left to right: Lt A.W. Hardwick (King's Colour), CSM Burke, Lt N.C. McPherson (Regimental Colour). RSM H.F. Tring DCM is centre back.

The 4th (Service) Battalion returning home from Mesopotamia on 19 August 1919. They are passing the Clarence in the Watton, Brecon. Marching behind the officers with and pace stick is RSM H.G. Staite.

The retirement of Pte John Williams VC from the SWB Depot Brecon staff on 26 May 1920. Pte Williams was awarded the VC for his action at the defence of Rorke's Drift on 22-3 January 1879 and rejoined the Regiment for the duration of the First World War. Left to right, back row: CMSI Edwards, CQMS Wilcox DCM, Col.-Sgt Lewis, Sgt Gibbs, Sgt Barnes, Sgt Sanders. Middle row: Sgt Dmr Sim, Ex-Sgt Dmr Davies, Sgt Marsh, Sgt Mason, CSM Bleasdale, Sgt Maher, Sgt Lamont, Ex-Sgt Rixon. Front row: CQMS Bowen, CSM Barker MM, RSM Bruntnell, Mr Atkins (probably 1300 Pte A Atkins 2/24th), Lt-Col. C.L. Taylor DSO, Pte J Williams VC, RQMS Woods MBE, CSM Wakefield, CSM Matthews, Col.-Sgt Lloyd.

The Regimental Polo team, Jhansi, 1921. Left to right: Capt. P.L. Villar MC, Lt-Col. Ll.G. Morgan Owen CMG CBE DSO, Capt. K.F.D. Gattie DSO MC, Maj. A.E. Williams DSO MC. Note the '24' polo shirts, the green pugeree on the helmet.

The laying up of Union Colours of the disbanded First World War Service Battalions – at SWB Depot Brecon before marching to Brecon Cathedral – on 25 May 1922. The Colours left to right are: 4th, 5th, 6th, 7th, 8th, 11th, 12th, 51st, 52nd and 53rd. The Union Colour of the 10th (1st Gwent) was laid up in Ebbw Vale parish church. It was on this day that the Havard chapel was designated as the Regimental Chapel of the South Wales Borderers.

The laying up of Union Colours of the disbanded First World War Service Battalions. The parade marches to the Cathedral on 25 May 1922 – Colonel of the Regiment, General Sir Alexander Cobbe VC is accompanied by Brig.-Gen. J.H. du B. Travers CB CMG, Brig.-Gen. B. Leach CB CMG and Lt-Col. A.J. Reddie CMG DSO.

The Wreath of Immortelles now on display in the Regimental Chapel in Brecon Cathedral.

The 2nd Battalion Annual Inspection, Barrackpore, India, with Lt-Col. T.C. Greenway (Commanding) on his horse, 1924.

1st Bn. THE WELSH GUARDS

(*Colours :* **WHITE**)

R WING KW

Gdsmn. Alexander
(1)

Lieut. W. Greenacre   Gdsmn. Arnold   Gdsmn. Nicholls   Gdsmn. Wait
(3)   (2)   (4)   (5)

Gdsmn. Morton   Gdsmn. Rees
(6)   (7)

Lieut. G. Young   Sergt. Pates   Gdsmn. Fisher   Gdsmn. Murphy   Gdsmn. Gibbons
(8) *Captain*   (9)   (10)   (11)   (12)

Gdsmn. Dunn   C/Sergt. Morgan   Corpl. Freeburg
(14)   (15)   (16)

Referee :   O   Major H. C. Harrison, D.S.O., M.C.

Corpl. C. Hughson   Pte. D. Lee   Lieut. T. C. Jones
(15)   (14)   (13)

Sergt. A. Vowles   Sergt. W. Hughson   Pte. G. Gully   Corpl. W. Thomas   Corpl. D. Jones
(12)   (11)   (10)   (9)   (8)

Sergt. W. Tippins   Pte. G. Daunt*r*
(7)   (6)

Dmr. W. Ward   Pte. I. Davies   Pte. D. Rees   Lieut. J. S. Windsor
(5)   (4)   (3) *LEFT CENTRE*   (2)   *LEFT WING*
RIGHT WING   R. CENTRE

Capt. C. A. Baker
(1) *Captain*

1st Bn. THE SOUTH WALES BORDERERS

TOUCH JUDGES : Capt. C. M. Usher, O.B.E., 2nd Bn. The Gordon Highlanders   Major Q. E. C. Partridge, The Welch Regiment.

PREVIOUS WINNERS & RUNNERS-UP IN THE ARMY RUGBY CUP COMPETITION.

Date.	Winners.	Runners-up.
1919-1920	2nd Battalion The Welch Regiment	2nd Life Guards
1920-1921	2nd Battalion The Welch Regiment	Training Battalion, Royal Engineers, Chatham
1921-1922	2nd Battalion The Welch Regiment	1st Battalion Gloucester Regiment
1922-1923	1st Battalion The Welsh Guards	2nd Battalion The Welch Regiment
1923-1924	2nd Battalion The Welch Regiment	1st Battalion The Welsh Guards
1924-1925	1st Battalion The South Wales Borderers	Royal Horse Guards (The Blues)

The programme for Army Rugby Cup Competition, 1925/6. 1st Battalion South Wales Borderers *v.* 1st Battalion Welsh Guards.

Spectators at the Army Rugby Cup semi-final – 1st Battalion Gloucester Regiment *v.* 1st Battalion South Wales Borderers – in 1925. The Borderers won 9-0 and went on to beat the Royal Horse Guards 16-3 in the Final that year.

The 1st Battalion South Wales Borderers *v.* 1st Battalion Welsh Guards in the Army Rugby Cup Competition 1925/6. The Borderers won 10-3.

Armistice Sunday at Brecon Cathedral in 1927. The Depot Representatives including Lt (later Maj.) A.G. Martin, Sgt Allen, Sgt Peate, Sgt Lowry.

The 2nd Battalion, Band and Corps of Drums, formed up in front of Agra Fort, India, 1927. Lt-Col. T.C. Greenway DSO is in command.

The building used as a temporary hospital during the defence of Rorke's Drift in 1879. Largely rebuilt, this photograph was taken in 1929 by a member of the 2nd Battalion.

Senior NCOs of the 1st (Rifle) Battalion the Monmouthshire Regiment receiving pay at annual camp in the 1920s. Although the Battalion was part of the Corps of South Wales Borderers, its members wore Rifle Brigade insignia.

Officers of the 1st (Rifle) Battalion, The Monmouthshire Regiment, at camp with Col. H.C.R. Thompson (Commanding) and Capt. P. Gottwaltz MC SWB (Adjutant) in 1929.

The Colour Party, 1st Battalion, at the Citadel, Cairo, in 1929. Seen with the Zulu war Colours are, left to right: Lt J.G. Richardson, Lt F.J. Billingham. Centre rear is RSM 'Slab' Norman DCM.

The Regimental Crest of 2nd Battalion on the main road to the Crater, Aden, in 1929. The crest commemorates the 2nd Battalion's visits to Aden 1892-3 and 1927-9. The crest was painted by Pioneer Sgt Kelly under the direction of Capt. (QM) J. Mellsop OBE prior to the departure of the 2nd Battalion in January 1929. The 1st Battalion were sent Aden during emergency of 1967. Today, the Crest is good order and the only British one remaining. There is a suggestion that the sphinx has some mystical powers.

The Colonel of the Regiment, General Sir Alexander Cobbe VC GCB KCSI DSO, on his way to unveil the South Wales Borderers memorial at Gheluvelt, near Ypres, 5 May 1929.

The Band of the 2nd Battalion, Portsmouth, 1930. Left to right, back row: Bdsm Wilson, Bdsm Butler, Bdsm Ricketts, Bdsm Richards, Bdsm Adams, Bdsm Hopkins, Bdsm Campbell, Bdsm Read, Bdsm Pewtner, Bdsm Roper. Middle row: Bdsm Briggs, Bdsm Brown, Bdsm Hunt, Bdsm Price, Bdsm Tofield, L/Cpl Price, Bdsm Hands, Bdsm Flynn, Bdsm Bidgood, L/Cpl Flower, Bdsm Taylor, Bdsm Wakelin. Front row: Bdsm Fredericks, Cpl McClear, L/Cpl McMillan, Bandmaster G.H. Willcocks LRAM ARCM, Band Sgt Talmage, Bdsm Gibbons, Bdsm Taylor Bdsm Hughes. Bandmaster Willcocks later became Director of Music, Irish Guards.

The 1st Battalion marching past HE The Governor of Hong Kong on 3 June 1931, the anniversary of the King's birthday. Left to right: 2nd-Lt J.O. Crewe-Read (Regimental Colour), RSM Norman, followed by 'C' Company, Lt H.M. Davies, Lt J.C. Richardson.

The Band programme for the 2nd Battalion Band at the Parade Bandstand, Worthing, between 31 May and 6 June 1931. The Battalion was stationed at Portsmouth at the time and the Band was constantly in demand to entertain South Coast holidaymakers with three concerts a day!

Borough of Worthing.

PARADE BANDSTAND.

ENTERTAINMENTS MANAGER ... F. H. COOPER.

May 31st to June 6th.

Week-days at 11.15 a.m., 3 & 7.45 p.m.
(Friday afternoons excepted).
Sundays at 3 & 8 p.m.

Band of H.M. 2nd Batt. The

South Wales Borderers

(24TH REGT.)

(By kind permission of Lt.-Col. G. H. Birkett, D.S.O., (Commanding) and Officers.)

CONDUCTOR :—

Mr. G. H. WILLCOCKS,

A.R.C.M. (Bandmaster).

W. A. NOICE, PRINTER, WORTHING.

Left to right: former CSM Jack Williams VC, DCM, MM, and former Pte John Williams VC outside the Guard Room, Brecon Barracks, at the Comrades' reunion on 15 May 1932. Jack Williams won his VC with the 10th Battalion (1st Gwents) in 1918. John Williams was awarded his VC for his gallant actions at Rorke's Drift with 'B' Company 2/24th on 22-3 January 1879.

73

The old and new Colours and the original Wreath of Immortelles after the presentation of Colours by HE The Governor, Sir William Peel KCMG KBE, on Hong Kong Racecourse on Tuesday 28 March 1933.

The new Colours of the 1st Battalion being marched off parade at Hong Kong Racecourse on Tuesday 28 March 1933. Left with the King's Colour is Lt A.J. Stocker and on the right with the Regimental Colour is Lt J.O. Crewe-Read. The names of the remainder of the Colour Party are not known.

The 1st Battalion, 1st, 2nd and 3rd soccer XIs in Hong Kong 1932/3. Left to right, back row: Williams 72, Williams 21, Mountford, Jones, John 75, Pritchard, Smith 08, Hazlewood, Marshfield, Addison, Nelson. Second row from the back: -?-, Matthais, Duncan, Fortey, Rees, Roberts 80, Harris 55, Wallace, Bebbington, Podmore, Wayes, Court, Jones 92. Third row, sitting: Lloyd, Capt. G.C. Cooper, Underwood, Lt-Col. G.T. Raikes DSO (Commanding), Suter, Mullane, Morrison. Front row: Hamblyn, Morris, Tex Williams, Harris. The cups are, left to right: Runners-Up Senior Shield, Runners-Up Junior Shield, Winners 3rd Division League.

The 2nd Battalion veterans of Tsingtao (from 1914) and the landing at Gallipoli (from 1915) at Catterick Camp in 1933. Left to right, back row: CSM A.H.S. MacFarlane, Sgt G.W. Saggers, Sgt A.E. Kelly, CQMS A. Thomas. Front row, seated: Lt-Col. G.H. Birkett DSO (Commanding), Maj. M.C. Morgan MC.

Marching off the Colours, 1st Battalion at Kudana Camp, India in 1936. The officers are wearing black crape armbands in mourning for the death of King George V.

The wedding of Lt J.W. Hope and Miss V. Campbell in Hong Kong on 22 February 1934, with Lt-Col. G.T. Raikes alongside.

The laying up Zulu war Colours (1st/24th) at Brecon Cathedral on 1 April 1934. Lt R.S. Cresswell (King's Colour) is on the left and Lt J.O. Crewe-Read (Regimental Colour) is on the right. The parade was commanded by Captain O.M. Wales MC.

Lt-Col. G.T. Raikes DSO, the Commanding Officer of 1st Battalion from 6 December 1931 to 21 April 1934. Commissioned in 1903, Geoffrey Raikes had distinguished service in the First World War being awarded a DSO and two bars. After retiring from the Army, he was appointed Lord Lieutenant for Brecknockshire. He was knighted in 1960.

The 2nd Battalion re-enact the Defence of Rorke's Drift at the Northern Command Tattoo, Ravensworth Castle, Gateshead under the direction of Captain H.M.StJ. Carpendale MC, 7-14 July 1934.

Veterans of the Zulu war visiting Northern Command Tattoo, Ravensworth Castle, Gateshead in July 1934 when the 2nd Battalion recreated the famous defence at Rorke's Drift: left to right ex-Pte A. Saxty (Newport), ex-Pte C. Wood (Nottingham), Lt.-Col F. Bourne OBE DCM (Dorking), Capt H.M.StJ. Carpendale MC, ex-Pte J. Jobbins (Pontypool), ex-Pte W. Cooper (Midhurst).

Warrant Officers and Sergeants of the 1st Battalion, Hong Kong, 1934. Left to right, back row: Sgt Ford, Sgt Beeson, Sgt Shaw, Sgt Richards, Sgt Underwood, Sgt Dean, Sgt Denton, Sgt Church, Sgt Hughes, Sgt Bradley, Sgt Varty, Sgt Witt, Sgt Vowles, Sgt Rallison. Second row from the back: Sgt Rice, Sgt Pallister, Sgt Weaver, Sgt Randle, Sgt Higgs, Sgt Thomas, Sgt Gaywood, Sgt Gould, Sgt Organ, Sgt Francis, Sgt Makepeace, Sgt Pritchard, Sgt Harvey, Sgt Facer. Third row: Sgt Bullimore, Sgt Todman, Sgt Bromley, Sgt Harnden, Col.-Sgt Horne, Col.-Sgt Griffiths, Col.-Sgt Hyde, Col.-Sgt Derry, Col.-Sgt Smith, Sgt Davies, Sgt Giddy, Sgt Smith, Sgt Smith. Front row: CSM Conway, CSM Nutt, CSM Lewis, Maj. R.G. Lochner MC, RSM O. Theobald, Lt-Col. G.T. Raikes DSO (Commanding), RQMS Henson, Captain H.M. Davies (Adjutant), ORQMS I. Jarman, Lt W.K. Miller (Quartermaster), CSM Brown.

Nine adjutants of the 2nd Battalion at Annual Comrades Reunion at Brecon on 1 April 1934. Left to right, back row: V.J.L. Napier, P.L. Villa, D.C. Campbell-Miles, R.I. Sugden. Front row: K.F.D. Gattie, G.H. Birkett, A.E. Williams, D.H.S. Somerville, O.M. Wales.

The Royal Salute of the 1st Battalion for the King's Birthday Parade in Hong Kong in 1934.

The 2nd Battalion Group in Malta in 1935. Those present include: Pte Allen, Pte McCann, Pte Swain, Cpl Duncan, L/Cpl Morgan and Pte Thomas.

Col. A.E. Williams DSO MC (Commanding), 1st Battalion, 1934-37. Aubrey Williams was commissioned to South Wales Borderers in 1907. He retired as a Major General in 1941.

The 1st Battalion on the march from Ghariom to Dosalli on 28 October 1937.

Left to right: Capt. H.M. Davies (Adjutant), Lt-Col. A.E. Williams DSO MC (Commanding), and Maj. P. Gottwaltz MC in India, 1937. Major Gottwaltz is wearing a Bombay Bowler.

The presentation of the Military Medal to L/Sgt J Roberts, 1st Battalion, by General Sir John Coleridge KCB CMG DSO, GOC-in-C Northern Command, India, at Ghariom Camp, Waziristan in 1938.

Five

The Second World War
1939-1945

South Wales Borderers

Twenty Battle Honours of which ten are worn on the Queen's Colour: NORWAY 1940, NORTH AFRICA 1942, NORTH-WEST EUROPE 1944-45, BURMA 1944-45, MAYU TUNNELS, NORMANDY LANDING, SULLY, CAEN, LE HAVRE, PINWE.

1st Battalion

On internal security duties in India until November 1941, when proceeded to Iraq joining 20th Indian Brigade, 10th Indian Division. Moved to Libya in May 1942. After heavy losses in retreat from Libya, the remnants of the Battalion went to Cyprus in 4th Indian Division. Battalion was disbanded in August 1942. Cadre went home to join 4th Battalion, The Monmouthshire Regiment, which became 1st Battalion The South Wales Borderers. Remained in England throughout the rest of the war, employed first on coast defence, then on garrison duty in the Orkneys from 1943 to 1944, and finally from 1944 to 1945 served as a special unit for training AA gunners as Infantrymen.

2nd Battalion

Moved to Barnard Castle in October 1939. Sent to Northern Norway in 24th Guards Brigade and took part in the Narvik campaign, April 1940. Evacuated from Norway and proceeded to Ulster in June 1940. Returned to England, December 1941. Served as an experimental unit for a Tank Brigade, 1942. Joined 9th Armoured Division, 1943. Transferred to 56th Independent Brigade, March 1944. Landed in Normandy on D-Day (6th June 1944) and fought with this Brigade through France, Belgium and Holland. Joined 158th Brigade 53rd (Welsh) Division on the Elbe in April 1945. Ended the war in Hamburg. Remained with the Army of Occupation until November 1946, when returned home. Passed into suspended animation in 1947. Disbanded in 1948.

5th Battalion

Raised in 1940 and served as a Home Defence unit consisting of men over thirty-five or unfit. Served in Newport until disbanded in 1943.

6th Battalion

Raised in Breconshire July 1940. Joined 212th Infantry Brigade in Lincolnshire in February 1941. Became 158th Regiment RAC in July 1942. Arrived in India, December 1942. Re-converted to infantry and joined 72nd Brigade, 36th Division, 1943. Joined 14th Army fighting in Burma in February 1944. Fought in the Burma campaign until the Japanese defeat was assured. Returned to India to join 71st Indian Infantry Brigade, 26th Indian Division May 1945 and was sent to Sumatra as part of re-occupation forces where engaged in operations against Indonesian Nationalists from October 1945 until March 1946.

7th Battalion

Raised in 1940 and trained as an infantry until 1943 when it was transferred to the Royal Artillery as a Light Anti-Aircraft Regiment and left the South Wales Borderers. In this capacity it served in North Africa and Italy.

1st Brecknockshire Battalion

Formed out of the 3rd Monmouths and Mobilized in 38th (Welsh) Division. Employed on Coast Defence and used as a draft finding unit until disbanded in July 1944.

The Monmouthshire Regiment

Nineteen Battle Honours, of which ten are worn on the Queen's Colour: THE ODEN, BOURGUEBUS RIDGE, LE PERIER RIDGE, FALAISE, ANTWERP, THE LOWER MAAS, THE OUTHE, THE RHINELAND, IBBENBUREN, THE ALLER.

2nd Battalion

Mobilized with 53rd (Welsh) Division and went to Caerphilly. In October 1939 proceeded to Northern Ireland returning in 1941. Proceeded to Normandy late June 1944, in 53rd (Welsh) Division (2nd Army). With this division took part in the campaign through France, Belgium, Holland and Germany. Served in the Army of Occupation in Germany until November 1945, when proceeded to Italy. Disbanded September 1946, but re-constituted in 1948.

3rd Battalion

Mobilized with 159th Brigade in 53rd (Welsh) Division. In April 1940, proceeded to Northern Ireland. Returned 1941. The Brigade became a Lorried Infantry in 29th Brigade of 11th Armoured Division in 1942 and landed in Normandy with this division on 14 June 1944. They took part in some of the heaviest fighting of the campaign in North-west Europe, moving through France, Belgium, Holland and Germany. Owing to heavy casualties the battalion was transferred to 115th Independent Infantry Brigade on the Rhine in April 1945. Remained in the Army of Occupation until passed into suspended animation in February 1946.

4th Battalion

Formed out of the 2nd Monmouths and Mobilized with 38th (Welsh) Division. In February 1942, the Anti-Aircraft platoon took part in a raid on the French coast. The Battalion was absorbed in the 1st Battalion, The South Wales Borderers, in December 1942.

Home Guard

Local Defence Volunteers created in May 1940. Brecknockshire units were affiliated to the South Wales Borderers and Monmouthshire units to the Monmouthshire Regiment.

South Wales Borderers Depot

Became 21st Infantry Training Centre serving all line regiments who normally recruited in Wales.

The 2nd Battalion returning to England aboard the SS *Franconia* after the ill-fated campaign in Norway, 6 June 1940. Interestingly, it was four years to the day when the 2nd Battalion returned to mainland Europe on D-Day.

The Band of the 3rd Battalion, The Monmouthshire Regiment, in Northern Ireland with Bandmaster A.H. Trotman in 1940.

3907897 PSM R.F. Richards (Cardiff) and 3906108 PSM W.G. Johnson (Newport), 2nd Battalion, after receiving their Distinguished Conduct Medals from HM The King at Buckingham Palace in 1941. They were decorated for their gallant actions during the 1940 Norway campaign.

Left: The 3in Mortar Platoon, 2nd Battalion, live firing at Rillington, Yorkshire, prior to the D-Day invasion in April 1943. *Right:* Maj. John Boon of the 2nd Battalion in 1943. John Boon wrote the history of the battalion's campaign through North West Europe, but he probably better known as the Director of Mills & Boon, the publishers of love stories.

Below opposite: Warrant Officers and Sergeants, 2nd Battalion, The Monmouthshire Regiment, at Sittingbourne, Kent, in October 1942. Left to right, back row: Sgt W.R. Stratford, Sgt W.C.E. Salmon, Sgt V. Crisp, Sgt B. Twining (RAOC), Sgt W.C. Booth, Sgt J. Woodhouse, L/Sgt Docking, Sgt G.S. Coleman (APTC), Sgt J. Ryan (ACC), Sgt C.W. Manning, L/Sgt M.J. McClenchy, CQMS E.L.Westcott. Middle row: Sgt R. Christian, CQMS W.A. Garmston, Sgt T. Morris, Sgt J. Wilmot, CQMS T. Watkins, Sgt W.J. Williams, Sgt W.A. Preston, Bandmaster W.H. Maynard, Sgt B.J. Hill, Sgt R. Adams, Sgt R. Martin, Sgt E. Jones, CQMS G.R. Price, ORS B.H. Carr. Front row: CSM R.E. Powell, CSM W.M. Ward, CSM C. Page, Capt. G.F.K. Morgan (Adjutant), RQMS A.T. Smith, Lt-Col. J.A. Garnons-Williams, RSM E.J. Morris, Maj. W.F.H. Kempster (Second in Command), CSM G. Musto, Lt W.H. Bailey (Quartermaster), CSM P. Jones, ORQMS D.W. Griffiths.

The 3in Mortar Platoon, 2nd Battalion, live firing at Rillington, Yorkshire, prior to the D-Day invasion in April 1943.

A practice river crossing, 2nd Battalion, at Consett, County Durham, prior to the D-Day invasion in January 1943.

A sketch of the original bridge over the River Kwai built by allied prisoners of war from 1943. This is from an original drawing by W.C. Wilder, drawn while a prisoner of war, which was presented to the regiment by 3908696 John Mills, 6th Battalion.

A prisoner of war camp in Burma in 1943. Once again, this is from an original drawing by W.C. Wilder presented by 3908696 John Mills 6th Battalion.

Officers of the 2nd Battalion, the Monmouthshire Regiment, at Salamanca Barracks, Aldershot, May 1944. Left to right, back row: Lt H.G. Smith, Lt D.A. Evans, Lt D. Nowell, Lt F.G. Ellis, Lt W.H. Bailey (QM), Lt L.M. Purvis, Lt J.W. Norman, Capt. D.M. Fairley, Lt R. Harrod, Lt S.A. Lucy, Lt F.S. Evans. Middle row: Lt F.L.S. Brown, Lt W.H. Perkins, Lt W.A. McIver, Lt T.W.A. Goddard, Lt A.R. Chubb, Lt A.D. Francis Williams, Lt F.V. Pearson, Lt O.T. Tucker, Lt J.L. Forsyth, Lt J.N. Scott, Revd H.C.C. Bowen CF, Lt G. Edwards. Front row: Capt. G.A. Weiss, Capt. J.D.P. O'Leary, Capt. Lt Gay, Maj. R.N. Deane, Maj. M. Williams, Maj. J. Price, Lt-Col. W.F.H. Kempster (Commanding), Capt. T.R. Baber, Maj. J.A. Chaston, Maj. G.F.K. Morgan, Capt. W.F.J. Hertbert, Capt. C. Harrison, Capt. G.N.S. Hughes.

A stretcher party, 3rd Battalion, The Monmouthshire Regiment, as part of the 11th Armoured Division, somewhere in Belgium, 1944. The censor has erased the 'Monmouthshire' shoulder titles.

Through Pagodaland – CSM A.J. Watkins MM (Abercarn) and Pte A. Lavell (Newport) going forward with their comrades of the 6th Battalion through Bahe in Burma in 1944.

The 6th Battalion after the capture of the Mayu Tunnels on 27 March 1944.

Left to right: Sgt Jack Lavis, Pte Reg Pugh and Pte Dai Price of the 6th Battalion in Burma in 1944.

The 2nd Monmouths, as part of 53rd Welsh Division, advancing through the snows in the Ardennes to La Roche, December 1944.

The 2nd Battalion, as part of 56th Independent Brigade, at Southampton prior to embarking for the D-Day landing on 6 June 1944. The South Wales Borderers was the only Welsh infantry unit to land in France on D-Day. The soldiers' cap badges have been removed by the censor.

Field Marshal Sir Claude Auchinleck, Commander-in-Chief in India, inspecting the 71st Indian Infantry Brigade including the 6th Battalion, at Bangalore on 3 September 1945. Members of the Battalion are wearing their famous pork pie hats. Closest to the camera is CQMS Croker who was awarded a DCM for his actions at Gyobin Chaung on 16 November 1944.

Cpl Edward Chapman of Pontlottyn who won the Victoria Cross while serving with 3rd Battalion, the Monmouthshire Regiment, at the Teutoburger Wald in April 1945. After the war, Ted Chapmen re-enlisted into the Territorials and reached the rank of Company Sergeant Major. For his devoted service he was awarded the BEM in the Coronation Honours of 1953.

Lt-Col. R.S. Cresswell taking the salute at the 6th Battalion parade in Samatra in 1946.

Six
The Final Chapter
1945-1969

South Wales Borderers

1st Battalion
Haifa, Palestine (1945-1946) – Famagusta, Cyprus (1946-1949) – Khartoum, Sudan (1949-1950) – Asmara, Eritrea (1950-1952) – Sennybridge, Brecknockshire (1952-1953) – Brunswick, Germany (1953-1955) – Brecon (1955) – Malaya Emergency (1955-1958) – Brecon (1958-1959) – (New Colours at Ebbw Vale: 25 July 1958) – Minden, Germany (1959-1962) – Worcester (1962-1963) – Hong Kong (1963-1966) – Lydd, Kent (1966-1967) – Aden emergency (1967) – Lydd, Kent (1967-1969) – Amalgamated with the Welch Regiment to form the 1st Battalion, The Royal Regiment of Wales (on 11 June 1969).

2nd Battalion
Solingen, Germany (1946) – Wüppertal, Germany(1946) – Malvern, Worcestershire (1946-1947) – Rorke's Drift Day – Battalion's last parade (1947).

The Monmouthshire Regiment TA

2nd Battalion
Re-constituted in 1948. (New Colours presented at Ebbw Vale on 25 July 1958). Continued to serve as part of Territorial Army until 1967 when only one company was retained in new TAVR as part of a NATO committed 'Welsh Volunteers' Battalion.

The Band and Drums, 1st Battalion, on parade at Caraolos Camp, Cyprus, June 1948.

'B' Company, 1st Battalion, marching past in Asmara, Eritrea, on Empire Day, June 1949. Left to right: Maj. K.D.C. Taylor, Capt. G.H. Briffett, RSM G.L. Friend, Lt R.P. Smith, 2nd-Lt L.A.H. Napier.

A 1st Battalion Signals Officer, Lt R.P. Smith, at TAC HQ during operations against the 'Shifta' in Eritrea, February 1950. Bob Smith later became curator of the South Wales Borderers Museum.

A typical South Wales Borderers' bed space, *c*. 1950.

RSM 'Killer' Richards sharing his keen interest in music with young George Sumsion in 1952. Eddie Richards acquired the sobriquet 'Killer' as he was a noted army boxer. He once fought the American Ezzard Charles – who later became World Heavywight Champion.

The 1st Battalion Coronation Colour Party on 2 June 1953. Left to right, back row: Cpl C.W. Savage, Sgt J. Newman, Lt P.J.R. Poncia, L/Cpl W.J. Danahar, 2nd-Lt G.D.G. Isaac (incorrectly dressed!), Sgt R. Blewitt, Pte R. Northy. Front row, seated: RSM L.C. Wood MBE, Maj. R.E.C. Price, Col.-Sgt L.G. Morgan.

Left to right: Lt G.J. Evans, Lt Peter Poncia and Capt. Alun Gwynne Jones enjoying a quick brew in Eritrea in 1952. Capt 'Alun' Gwynne Jones is better known today as Lord Chalfont.

HM The Queen meeting Sgt Edward Chapman VC BEM at Newport during the Coronation visit to the Borough in July 1953. The Guard of Honour was provided by 2nd Monmouths and commanded by Major HC Roberts. (Photograph courtesy of *South Wales Argus*)

A visit of Lt-Gen. Sir Lashmer Whistler KBE CB DSO to the SWB Depot, Brecon, on 18 February 1954. Those present include: Maj. (QM) W.G. Lewis, Lt-Col. E.N.G. Earle, and Recruit R. Patterson.

The visit of HM The Queen to Brecon, August 1955. Left to right: Maj. B.W.T. Elliott (Guard Commander), CSM I.V. Warburn (Right Guard), Lt G.D.C. Isaac (Subaltern), 2nd-Lt J.A.P. Hollis (Ensign).

The 1st Battalion embarking aboard SS *Dilwara* for Malaya, September 1955. Lt R.H. Godwin-Austen is seen counting numbers.

Operation 'Kingly Pile' in Malaya on 21 February 1956. Left to right: an unknown civilian, 2nd-Lt M.H. Wheaton, Sgt A.B. Pozzi, Maj. R.N. Deane MC, Lt-Col. R.C.H. Miers DSO OBE, Evan Davies, Maj. J.E. Magesson MBE, Police Inspector Wee, Cpl Chivers.

Internal Security Operations by the 1st Battalion, Singapore, November 1956. Note the 'XXIV' on the steel helmets.

'Cheese', left to right: RSM J. Martell MBE, Capt. P.J.R. Poncia, Lt-Col. R.C.H. Miers DSO OBE (Commanding), snapped in Malaya in 1957.

Lt-Col. R.C.H. Miers DSO OBE (Commanding) receiving the salute from the 1st Battalion Quarter Guard at the Commander-in-Chief's Residence, Malaya, 1956. The duty drummer is using one of the 1908 silver side drums.

Left to right: Cpl Powell, Sgt Beese and 2nd-Lt G.H. Roblin in Malaya, 1957. Graham Roblin later became a Army Padre and retired as Assistant Chaplain General.

Corned beef or spam for the 2nd Monmouths at Windmill Hill, Salisbury Plain, in 1957.

The Band and Drums rehearsing the 'troop' for the Colours Parade, Brecon, July 1958.

The Colour Parties of 1st, 2nd and 3rd (Militia) Battalions at the lychgate of Brecon Cathedral for the laying-up of the Colours, Sunday 14 September 1958. RSM J. Martell MBE is seen leading the Colour parties.

The last Regimental Colour of 1st Battalion, being presented at Ebbw Vale by HRH The Duke of Edinburgh KG on 25 July 1958.

The last Queen's Colour of the 1st Battalion being presented at Ebbw Vale by HRH The Duke of Edinburgh KG on 25 July 1958.

The presentation of new Colours at Ebbw Vale on 25 July 1958. HRH The Duke of Edinburgh KG, who stood in for the Queen, is accompanied by Lt-Col. R.O. Crewe-Read MC (Parade Commander).

The presentation of new Colours at Ebbw Vale on 25 July 1958. HRH The Duke of Edinburgh meets Mrs J. Williams, widow of CSM 'Jack' Williams VC DCM MM. Standing next to Mrs Williams is In-Pensioner J. Williams, formerly Sgt SWB. The Colonel of the Regiment, Maj.-Gen. F.R.G. Matthews CB DSO looks on.

Great Western 'Castle' Class Locomotive No 4037 in 1957. It was named 'The South Wales Borderers' at an unveiling ceremony held at Paddington station by Maj.-Gen. Ll.G. Morgan-Owen CB CMG CBE DSO, Colonel of the Regiment on 14 April 1937. The locomotive was taken out of service in 1962, at which time the number and name plates were presented to the SWB Museum by British Railways. The last occasion on which the locomotive was used to carry passengers was in June 1959, when it conveyed the 1st Battalion on part of their journey to Minden, Germany. Lt-Col. P.J. Martin and Maj. B.M. Pim are seen here waiting to board the train at Hereford.

The re-badging parade at Clifton Barracks, Minden, in 1960. On 2 April 1960 the 1st Battalion adopted the Welsh Brigade capbadge (i.e. The Prince of Wales's feathers). Here Lt-Col. Martin (Commanding Officer) is seen inspecting the new Badge Guard with Maj. W.J. Parsons MBE (Guard Commander) followed by Capt. P.M. Pim (Adjutant).

1st Battalion Regimental Quarter Guard at Minden found from the Mortar Platoon on 4 December 1959.

Afternoon surgery, the Blenheim March, 18 July-12 August 1961. 'B' Company re-traced the 400 miles covered by the Duke of Marlborough in 1704. The Duke was Colonel of the 24th at the time. 2nd-Lt S.R.A. Stocker is seen inspecting the feet of Ptes Howells 44, Vokes, Hext, Lloyd 21 (leg up), Price 51, Clavey 74 and Jayne.

Warrant Officers and Sergeants, 1st Battalion, Clifton Barracks, Minden, 1961. Left to right, back row: Sgt Eustace, Sgt Morgan, Sgt V. Lloyd, Sgt Tuckwell REME, Sgt Beese, Sgt K. Morris, Sgt Jones 93, Sgt Cleverly, Sgt Smith 32, Sgt Meredith, Sgt Bailey ACC, Sgt Hocking, Sgt Pryce, Sgt North. Second row from the back: Sgt Lambert, Sgt Ball, Sgt Crabb, Sgt Cox RAPC, Sgt Pennington, Sgt Button, D/Maj. Davies, Sgt John, Sgt Bromage, Sgt Marshall, Sgt Doren, Sgt Wakefield, Sgt Newman. Third row: CSM Mandle, CSM Turner, Sgt Pitchford, Col.-Sgt Burnell, Col.-Sgt Jenkins, Col.-Sgt Morris, S/Sgt Wilkinson REME, CSM Hamlin, S/Sgt Fildes RAPC, Col.-Sgt Pozzi, Col.-Sgt Sumsion, Col.-Sgt Carter, Col.-Sgt O'Connor, WOII Landy BEM, CSM Mackrell. Front row: CSM Wilkey, Lt F.S. Field, Band S.M. Reed, Capt. C.J. Lee, ASM Oakley BEM, Lt-Col. A.K. Sharp, RSM Warburn, Maj. B.W.T. Elliott, Bandmaster Whiting, Capt.(QM) H.T. Welling, RQMS King, CSM Chandler, CSM Holland.

CQMS 'Chef' Carter with the menu for the day at Sennelager in 1961. Crow stew?

The 1st Battalion Rorke's Drift Ball, Minden, 1962. Left to right: Lt-Col. A.K. Sharp (commanding), Mr Ivor Rees VC, Maj.-Gen. D. Peel Yates (Colonel of the Regiment), Mr Edward Chapman VC, RSM I. Warburn.

Brothers serving with the 1st Battalion, November 1962. Left to right, back row: Pte G. Clavey, Pte F.J. Cavey (Swansea), L/Cpl A. Readon (Risca), Pte W. Readon (Abertillery), Bdsm B.N. Wood, Bdsm M.J. Wood (York). Second row from the back: L/Cpl D.G. Davies, Cpl R.T. Davies, Pte F. Davies, Cpl H. Davies (Tredegar). Third row: Pte G. Fowler, Cpl T. Fowler (Thornaby-on-Tees), Bdsm M.J. Price, Dmr W. Price (Merthyr). Front row: Sgt D.J. Carter (Swansea), Col.-Sgt K. Carter (Brecon), Sgt K. Griffiths, Pte A. Griffiths (Pontypridd).

Farewell to National Service in 1962. To mark the end of National Service, the last sixty-four National Servicemen parade as a separate company under command of Maj. John Evans at the Annual Inspection by the Brigade Commander in Minden.

The new Commanding Officer and Regimental Sergeant Major of the 1st Battalion, Lt-Col. 'Tim' Evill and RSM Des Webb, settle in together at Norton Barracks, Worcester, in 1963.

1st Bn South Wales Borderers
XXIV XXIV
Wos And Sgts Mess

WO1 D WEBB R.S.M.   WO1 O.R. WHITING B/M

WO11 W.A.KING	SGT K.MORRIS	QMSL J.HOOKER
WO11 D.SMITH	SGT T.V.LLOYD	SGT R.JOHNSON
WO11 R.W.HOLLAND	SGT E.J.SHORT	SGT D.J.CARTER
WO11 P.M.ANDEL	SGT A.BALL	SGT D.T.HARKETT
WO11 R.G.HAMLIN	SGT R.A.CRABB	SGT M.EUSTAGE
WO11 A.B.POZZI	SGT R.JONES	SGT J.GREGORY
WO11 J.O'CONNOR	SGT K.BROWN	SGT G.HOCKING
WO11 J.NEWMAN	SGT T.J.JONES	SGT D.BUTTON
WO11 R.LANDY B.E.M	SGT N.G.PRYCE	SGT D.V.GILLARD
CSGT R.J.MACCORMACK	SGT B.JAMES	SGT J.LEAHY
CSGT C.MYNEHAN	SGT D.C.BAKER	SGT K.O.GRIFFITHS
CSGT J.MURPHY	SGT D.JOHN	SGT W.MEREDITH
CSGT K.CARTER	SGT K.MORRIS	SGT L.FREEMAN
CSGT H.R.DAVIES	SGT H.DAVIES	SGT H.BROMAGE
CSGT N.CLEVERLEY	SGT D.R.ELLIS	SGT G.SULLIVAN
CSGT J.JENKINS	SGT J.GGOULD	S/SGT F.WILKINSON
CSGT C.BURNELL	SGT W.BAILEY	S/SGT R.FILDES
CSGT T.WAKEFIELD	SGT D.C.SMITH	SGT K.ALMOND

Hongkong   1963

Warrant Officers' and Sergeants' Mess, 1st Battalion, Hong Kong, 1963.

HM the Queen Mother, Queen Elizabeth, inspecting the Guard of Honour provided by 'C' Company, 1st Battalion, on the occasion of her visit to the Isle of Man to open the Annual Tynwald Hill ceremony on the Friday 5 July 1963. The Queen Mother is accompanied by Capt. N.O. Roberts (Guard Commander).

Lt David Richards (right) with his 2nd Monmouths team in the Cambrian March Competition, September 1963. The team includes, left to right: Sgt Jones, L/Cpl Crees, Pte Parker, Pte James, Pte Forsey. Lt Richards, Ptes Parker, James and Forsey continued their TA service with the 3rd Volunteer Battalion, The Royal Regiment of Wales.

RSM Joe Whitehead about to taste the champagne in June 1963. The 2nd Monmouths had just won the Major Units Championship at the 53rd Welsh Division Small Arms Meeting.

HM the Queen meeting Recruit John Husein (Newport) at the opening of the new Welsh Brigade Depot at Cwrt-y-Gollen, Crickhowell, on 10 May 1963. Rct Husein prospered and (now a Major) is one of the last members of the South Wales Borderers still serving in the Royal Regiment of Wales. The Queen is accompanied by Gen. Sir Hugh Stockwell GCB KBE DSO, Colonel of The Royal Welch Fusiliers.

A Royal Salute by a Tri-Service Guard of Honour is given to HE Sir Robert Black GCMG OBE, the retiring Governor of Hong Kong in 1964. The Governor is accompanied by Lt-Gen. Sir Richard Craddock KBE CB DSO, (late Buffs) who commanded 2/SWB on D-Day. In front of the Guard are: Maj. H.R. Williams (Commanding), Lt A.B. Cole (Subaltern) and Lt T.M.E. Brown (Queen's Colour).

Lt Bob Hitch and Cpl H. Hook with the manager of Paramount Films (Hong Kong) at the Princess Theatre on 26 July 1964. They were present for the Hong Kong premier of *Zulu* in aid of the Army Benevolent Fund. Lt Hitch and Cpl Hook are both related to soldiers who won a Victoria Cross at Rorke's Drift.

The Colonel of the Regiment, the Commanding Officer and Adjutant with the Warrant Officers, 1st Battalion, Hong Kong, November 1964. Left to right: CSM T.R.J. MacCormack, CSM A.B. Pozzi, QMS I.J. Hooker (APTC), WO2 Anderson (ACC), CSM D. Smith, CSM R.G. Hamlin, Capt. T.M.E. Brown, Bandmaster O.R. Whiting, Lt-Col. A.R. Evill, Maj.-Gen. D. Peel Yates DSO OBE, CSM J. Newman, RSM R. Chandler, CSM Mandel, CSM W.A. King, CSM R. Wilkey.

The Quarter Guard – 'Hot but steady' for the visit of the Maj.-Gen. D.G. Lang CB DSO MC, Director of Army Training to the 1st Battalion, Hong Kong, 1964.

Soldiers of 'B' and 'C' Companies, 2nd Monmouths, board HMS *St David* at Cardiff Docks in 1964. HMS *St David* was a coastal minesweeper from the South Wales Division RNR and the soldiers were present for a weekend exercise, 'Pirates Nest', on Lundy Island in the Severn Estuary in May 1964. The soldiers were under command of Maj. David Williams QC, assisted by Capt. David Webber and Lt Nigel Eveleigh.

DWARFING THE MIGHTIEST! TOWERING OVER THE GREATEST!

JOSEPH E. LEVINE presents

ZULU

A STANLEY BAKER-CY ENDFIELD Production

starring

STANLEY **BAKER** · JACK **HAWKINS** · ULLA **JACOBSSON** · JAMES **BOOTH** · MICHAEL **CAINE**

Original Screenplay by JOHN PREBBLE and CY ENDFIELD
Suggested by an article written by JOHN PREBBLE
Directed by CY ENDFIELD
Original music composed and conducted by JOHN BARRY

TECHNICOLOR ® **TECHNIRAMA** ®

A DIAMOND FILMS Ltd. PRODUCTION · A PARAMOUNT RELEASE

Narration spoken by RICHARD BURTON

The front cover of the souvenir programme for the World Premiere of *Zulu* at the Plaza Theatre, London, on 22 January 1964.

The Colour Party, 1st Battalion, followed by No. 2 Guard commanded by Capt. Tom Brown marching past the His Excellency Sir David Trench KCMG MC, The Governor of Hong Kong, on the Queen's Birthday Parade on 2 April 1965.

The 1st Battalion hockey team, Hong Kong, 1965. Left to right, at the back: Cpl Shanahan, Back row, standing: Sgt Gregory, L/Cpl Evans, Bdsm Pembridge, QMSI Hooker (APTC), Sgt Brown, Capt. R.W. Isaac. Front row, sitting: Bdsm Barnes, Maj. L.A.H. Napier MC, Bandmaster O.R. Whiting, Band Sgt Wilding, L/Cpl Bush.

Pte Idris Richards (Maesteg), holder of the Far East Light Middleweight title, ABA title holder and Inter-Unit Championship title holder, sparring with L/Cpl Evans. Pte Richards, an APT instructor, toured Vietnam with the British Army display team. He also boxed for the Hong Kong Colony team against the Japanese Olympic team.

Brig. R.E.C. Price DSO (late SWB), acting Brigade Colonel, with Drummers Silver and Rafferty, followed by Lt-Col. A.R. Evill (Commanding) and Capt. T.M.E. Brown (Adjutant) in Hong Kong, December 1965.

1st Battalion Rugby XV, Hong Kong, 1965. Left to right, standing: Cpl Bevan, L/Cpl Matadigo, Pte Bowden, Capt A.B. Cole, Cpl Ralph, Sgt Hawkins, WO2 North, Pte Long, S/Sgt Harkett. Seated: Cpl Bush, Pte Freeman, Pte Jenkins 37, Sgt Freeman (team captain), Cpl Tabua, L/Cpl Kukuve, Sgt Addison.

The United Nations Honor Guard in Seoul, Korea, 22 April 1965. Ten members of the 1st Battalion were included in this particular guard. The officer is 2nd-Lt 'Jimmy' McSheehy.

Cpl Hook is showing Lieutenant Coghill's sword to newly joined members of the 1st Battalion in Hong Kong in 1965. Lt Coghill and Lt Melvill saved the Queen's Colour after Isandhlwana in 1879.

The Queen's Birthday Parade, Hong Kong, 21 April 1966. The 1st Battalion Colour Party is made up of, left to right: Lt S.R.A. Stocker (Queen's Colour), CSM North, Lt O.M. Roberts (Regimental Colour), Sgt K. Gill. They are seen marching past HE The Governor.

The 1st Battalion taking over Windsor Castle Guard from 2nd Battalion Coldstream Guards in October 1966. 2nd-Lt R.P. Hobart-Tichborne is commanding.

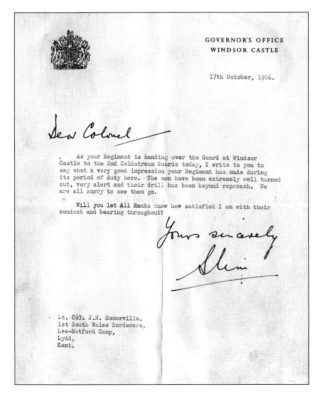

A copy letter of congratulation sent to the Commanding Officer, 1st Battalion, by the Governor of Windsor Castle, Field-Marshal The Viscount Slim KG, in 1966.

Against the backdrop of the Keep of Cardiff Castle, Ptes Wright and Scott of 'B' Company, 1st Battalion, rehearse one of the battle scenes to be staged as part of the Cardiff Searchlight Tattoo, August 1966.

CSM Gordon Amphlett (Merthyr) in good voice at Windsor Castle when the 1st Battalion took over the Castle Guard from the 2nd Battalion Coldstream Guards, 23 September 1966.

Former Sgt Ivor Rees VC telling young recruits about the First World War at Welsh Brigade Depot at Cwrt-y-Gollen, Chrickhowell, on the fiftieth anniversary of the battle of the Somme in July 1966.

The memorial gates at the 24th Regiment, South Wales Borderers' Museum, Brecon. They were unveiled, on 10 September 1967, by Capt. Lauchlan Rose MC, President 5th Battalion Association, to commemorate the service of Col. C.V. Trower CMG and the soldiers of the 5th (Pioneer) Battalion (1914-18).

The 1st Battalion Inter-Platoon Competition at Stanford Training Area, May 1968. 2nd-Lt Christopher Elliott is seen preparing his defences. Now Major-General Christopher Elliott, he is currently Colonel of the Royal Regiment of Wales.

Lt Ian Buchanan as 'Lt Gonville Bromhead VC', Cardiff Tattoo 1968. 'Have a break….' Lt Buchanan is the nephew of Capt. Angus Buchanan who was awarded the Victoria Cross for his gallant action in Mesopotamia in April 1916.

The re-creation of the defence of Rorke's Drift, 1879, by the 1st Battalion at the Cardiff Tattoo, 1968. In the centenary year of this famous action, the 1st Battalion the Royal Regiment of Wales also re-enacted the event at the 1979 Cardiff Tattoo.

A Guard of Honour found from No. 6 Platoon for the Lord Warden of the Cinque Ports, Lydd, 1968. The Rt Hon. Sir Robert Menzies KT, former Prime Minister of Australia, is greeted by 2nd-Lt Doug Sharp (Platoon Commander).

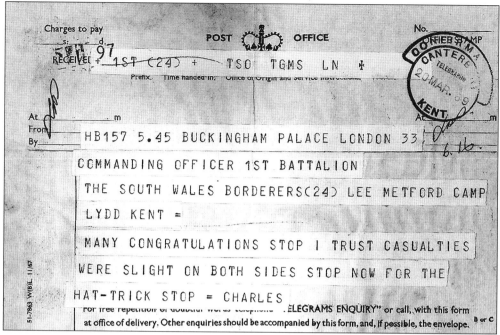

A copy congratulatory telegram sent by HRH the Prince of Wales to the 1st Battalion on winning the Army Rugby Union Challenge Cup in 1968/9.

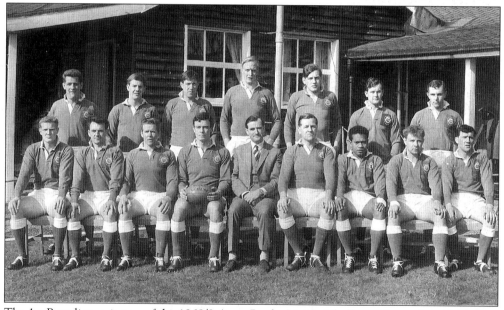

The 1st Battalion, winners of the 1968/9 Army Rugby Union Challenge Cup, a feat which they achieved for the fifth time. The Regiment beat 7th Signal Regiment, 11-3. Left to right, back row: Cpl J.J. O'Brien, Pte D.W. Chown, Sgt R.J. Ralph, Pte H. Rundle, 2nd-Lt D.M.J. Hodges, L/Cpl J. Lang, Cpl P.M. Beard. Front row: Cpl G. Boden, Pte J.W. Lewis, Cpl T. Coates, Lt T.L. Williams (team captain), Lt-Col. L.A.H. Napier MBE (Commanding), Maj. D.E. Cox, Cpl J. Kucuve, Cpl J.V. Jenkins, Pte G.D. Llewellyn.

The South Wales Borderers exercising their rights as Freemen of the County Borough of Newport for the last time on 7 June 1968. The Freedom of Newport was later granted to the Royal Regiment of Wales. The drummers are seen with the battalion's 1908 silver drums which had recently been converted to modern rod tensioning.

HRH the Prince of Wales KG, as Colonel-in-Chief, salutes the new Queen's Colour of 1st Battalion, The Royal Regiment of Wales (24th/41st Foot), at Cardiff Castle on 11 June 1969. The honour of a silver wreath, attached to the pike, was awarded to the 24th Regiment for their actions during the Zulu war. Receiving the new Colour is Lt P.D. Gordon. Handing over the Queen's Colour to the Colonel-in-Chief is Maj. I.D.B. Mennell.